MONTECARLO SIMULATION OF TWO COMPONENT AEROSOL PROCESSES

Authored by **Jose Ignacio Huertas**

Montecarlo Simulation of Two Component Aerosol Processes
http://dx.doi.org/10.5772/60735
Authored by Jose Ignacio Huertas

Contributors

Jose Ignacio Huertas

Published by InTech

Janeza Trdine 9, 51000 Rijeka, Croatia

Publishing Process Manager Danijela Duric

Technical Editor InTech DTP team

Cover InTech Design team

First published March, 2016

Printed in Croatia

Additional hard copies can be obtained from orders@intechopen.com

Montecarlo Simulation of Two Component Aerosol Processes, Authored by Jose Ignacio Huertas

p. cm.

Print ISBN 978-953-51-2262-3

Online ISBN 978-953-51-2263-0

For EU product safety concerns:
IN TECH d.o.o., Prolaz Marije Krucifikse Kozulić 3, 51000 Rijeka, Croatia,
info@intechopen.com or visit our website at intechopen.com.

Meet the author

Dr. Jose Ignacio Huertas: Mechanical engineer from Los Andes University, Colombia (1988). Doctor of Science from Washington University, St. Louis, USA (1997). Associate professor at Los Andes University until 2002. Currently, full time professor at Tecnológico de Monterrey, Mexico. Has leaded the Energy Research Group in Colombia and the Automotive Engineering Research Center-CIMA in Mexico. Has published 45 papers mainly related to combustion and air pollution. Has graduated 6 PhD and 61 MSc. students. Has completed 90 research projects financed by private companies and governmental institutions. Currently works as researcher of the Energy and Climate Change Group of the School of Science and Engineering at Tecnológico de Monterrey. Is member of the national system of researcher in both Mexico and Colombia.

Contents

Preface IX

Section 1 Introduction 1

Chapter 1 **Introduction 3**
Jose Ignacio Huertas

Section 2 Sodium/Halide Flame Synthesis of W and W-Ti Nanoparticles 15

Chapter 2 **Sodium/Halide Flame Synthesis of W and W-Ti Nanoparticles 17**
Jose Ignacio Huertas

Section 3 Modeling Aerosol Processes 35

Chapter 3 **Modeling Aerosol Processes 37**
Jose Ignacio Huertas

Section 4 Monte Carlo Simulation of Coagulating Aerosols 45

Chapter 4 **Monte Carlo Simulation of Coagulating Aerosols 47**
Jose Ignacio Huertas

Section 5 Condensation 67

Chapter 5 **Incorporating Condensation into the Markov-MC Model 69**
Jose Ignacio Huertas

Section 6 The Particle Encapsulation Process 83

Chapter 6 **The Particle Encapsulation Process 85**
Jose Ignacio Huertas

Section 7 Conclusions 109

Chapter 7 **Conclusions and Recommendations 111**
Jose Ignacio Huertas

Section 8 Appendix 121

Chapter 8 **Appendices 123**
Jose Ignacio Huertas

Preface

Nanophase materials also referred to as nanostructured, nanocrystalline, or nanometer-sized crystalline solids, are single-phase or multiphase polycrystals, with dimensions of the order of 1–100 nm. Compared to conventional materials, nanophase materials possess unique advantages with respect to properties and processing. As grain size decreases down to the nanometer-size range, nanophase metals generally get stronger and harder, while nanophase ceramics show ductility, even superplasticity, at lower temperatures than conventional brittle ceramics. For example, 1000% increase in fracture stress, 2000% increase in magnetic susceptibility, 25% decrease in density, and 165% improvement in critical temperature for superconductivity have been observed in nanophase metals.

The high-performance properties exhibited by nanophase materials have important implications for industry. For example, several tool companies are expected to introduce stronger, tougher, long-lasting cutting tools, drill bits, and wear parts composed of ultrafine grain cobalt/tungsten carbide composites. Some nanocomposites exhibit an unusual magnetic behavior called "giant magnetoresistance," which is being considered for read/write information in storage devices and to make improved magnetoresistive sensors. Another application under consideration is solid-state magnetic refrigerators based on the mega caloric effect by which heat is reversibly absorbed and discharged when small ferromagnetic particles are aligned by magnetic fields. In addition, unusual magneto-optical characteristics of nanostructured iron oxide are expected to be applicable for high definition color copiers.

This book describes a novel method for the production of high purity, unagglomerated nano-particulates of tungsten (W) and tungsten titanium alloys (W-Ti) by flame synthesis. These materials possess unique properties that make them desirable for advanced applications.

W-Ti nano-sized alloys have a combination of high strength (800–1000 MPa), high ductility (10–30%), good electrical and thermal conductivity, corrosion resistance, and excellent machinability. Current applications for W and W-Ti include counterbalances in military aircraft, radiation shields, lighting components, ignition electrode materials, catalysts in the chemical industry, alloying elements for high speed steels, sputter targets in VLSI chip technology, and a variety of sport related parts

Dr. Jose Ignacio Huertas
Tecnológico de Monterrey,
Mexico

Section 1

Introduction

Chapter 1

Introduction

Jose Ignacio Huertas

Additional information is available at the end of the chapter

http://dx.doi.org/10.5772/62024

1. Nanophase materials

More than 30 years ago, Nobel Prize–winning physicist Richard P. Feynman mused that in the future, when scientists have learned how to control the arrangement of matter on a very small scale, they would see materials take on an enormously richer variety of properties. [1] In recent years, considerable attention was focused on the production of these materials, so-called *nanophase materials*. These materials, also referred to as nanostructured, nanocrystalline, or nanometer-sized crystalline solids, are single-phase or multiphase polycrystals, with dimensions of the order of 1–100 nm. [1] They can be classified according to the number of dimensions of the grain in the nanometer range as shown in Table 1. A general review of nanophase materials is found in References 2 and 3.

Dimensionality	Designation	Typical method of synthesis
3D	Crystallites (equiaxed)	Gas condensation
2D	Filamentary	Chemical vapor deposition
1D	Layered (lamellar)	Electrodeposition

Table 1. Classification of nanophase materials.

Compared to conventional materials, nanophase materials possess unique advantages with respect to properties and processing. [4] As grain size decreases down to the nanometer-size range, nanophase metals generally get stronger and harder, while nanophase ceramics show ductility, even superplasticity, at lower temperatures than conventional brittle ceramics. For example, 1000% increase in fracture stress, 2000% increase in magnetic susceptibility, 25% decrease in density, and 165% improvement in critical temperature for superconductivity have been observed in nanophase metals. [5] As an example, Figure 1 shows the stress–strain curve for a) nanophase (14 nm) Pd sample compared with that for a coarse-grained (50 μm) Pd sample and b) nanophase (25 nm) Cu sample compared with that for a coarse-grained (50 μm)

Cu sample. [6] It shows that the yield stress for nanophase materials for these two materials is higher than the conventional material.

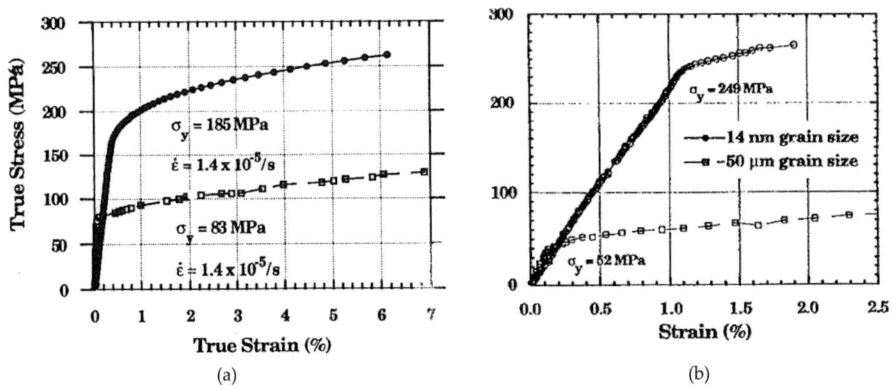

Figure 1. Stress–strain curve for a) nanophase (14 nm) Pd sample compared with that for a coarse-grained (50 μm) Pd sample, and b) nanophase (25 nm) Cu sample compared with that for a coarse-grained (50 μm) Cu sample. [6]

These unique properties arise because of the dramatic grain refinement and the novel characteristic of grain boundaries. Nanophase materials contain a high concentration of grain boundaries with random orientation, and consequently a substantial fraction of atoms lies in the interfaces. For example, when grain size is about 5 nm, there are approximately 10^{19} boundaries/cm^3 with random orientation and 50% volume fraction of atoms at the interfaces. The volume fraction decreases to about 30% for 10 nm grains and to about 3% for 100 nm grains. Figure 2 is a schematic representation of a nanophase metal. [7]

The increase in strength of nanophase materials stems from the smaller grain sizes, which cause a change in the fundamental mechanism of plastic deformation. In conventional metals, the fundamental mechanism is dislocation migration, [8] where rows of missing atoms within the lattice (dislocations) migrate in the direction opposite of an applied stress. The result of this migration is that dislocations pile up on one side of the grain, and thus the grains themselves are deformed. The ease of migration of these dislocation lines is related to the length of the dislocation line; longer lines migrate more readily than shorter lines. [9, 10]

In conventional metals where grain sizes are large, these dislocation lines are very long and consequently can migrate readily. In nanocrystalline materials where grain sizes are very small, the dislocation lines are very short, and do not migrate readily. Dislocation migration is then effectively shut down as a mechanism of plastic deformation in nanocrystalline materials. Grain boundary sliding becomes the active mechanism of deformation in nanocrystalline materials. This mechanism of plastic deformation does not cause deformation of the individual grains. It is a higher-energy mechanism of deformation, yielding increased strength in nanocrystalline metals, and for nanophase ceramics it provides a mechanism for plastic deformation that formerly was not present. The increased ductility in ceramics can be attributed to grain boundary sliding and the higher rates of atomic diffusion in the less dense grain boundaries as compared to the crystalline grains.

http://dx.doi.org/10.5772/62024

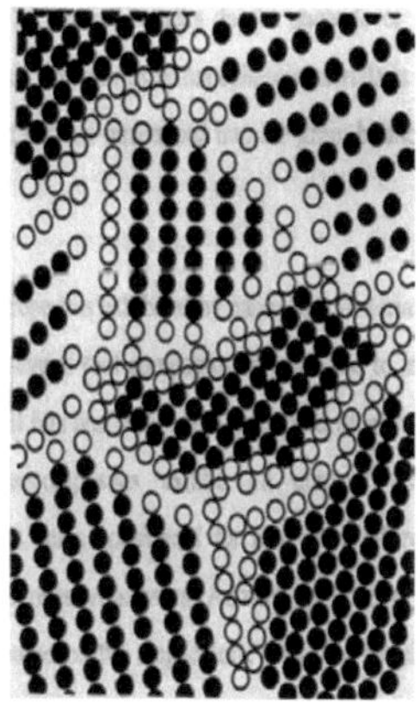

Figure 2. Schematic representation of an equiaxed nanocrystalline metal distinguishing between the atoms associated with the individual crystal grains (filled circles) and those constituting the boundary network (open circles). [11]

The improved facture toughness of nanophase materials is related to the increased grain boundary fraction. Fracture toughness is defined as the ability of a material to resist cracking. Cracks nucleate in areas of stress concentration, which includes areas where dislocations pile up. If stress concentration sites can be relieved, cracks do not nucleate or propagate. The advantage of the increased number of grain boundaries in nanophase materials is that the stress concentrations are relieved because dislocations are introduced into the grain boundaries more quickly, and therefore they do not pile up.

The high-performance properties exhibited by nanophase materials have important implications for industry. For example, several tool companies are expected to introduce stronger, tougher, long-lasting cutting tools, drill bits, and wear parts composed of ultrafine grain cobalt/ tungsten carbide composites. Some nanocomposites exhibit an unusual magnetic behavior called "giant magnetoresistance," which is being considered for read/write information in storage devices and to make improved magnetoresistive sensors. Another application under consideration is solid-state magnetic refrigerators based on the mega caloric effect by which heat is reversibly absorbed and discharged when small ferromagnetic particles are aligned by magnetic fields. In addition, unusual magneto-optical characteristics of nanostructured iron oxide are expected to be applicable for high definition color copiers. [12] Production of nanophase materials typically involves two steps: powder preparation and powder consolidation. To better appreciate the required specifications of the starting powders, we will consider powder consolidation first.

2. Consolidation

Advance materials are processed in a manner similar to traditional ceramics, i.e., by compacting and firing powders as illustrated in Figure 3. The process that often follows powder preparation involves dispersing the powders in solution by adding organic polymers or surfactants. These highly concentrated suspensions are called slurries, or slips.

The final shape of the material is given when the slurry is either poured in a form (slip casting), spread onto a smooth surface (tape casting), or coated on a support. It is currently recognized that powder packing, which occurs during this stage, determines the structures that deve1op during sintering. After drying, the material (called "green" before firing) is sintered at a temperature and pressure that depends on particle size, composition, and sintering aids. Nanophase materials must be compacted and sintered at temperatures low enough to prevent grain growth and at the same time high enough so that sufficient sintering occurs to form dense, uniform polycrystalline materials. Typically, nanophase powders are consolidated by vacuum hot pressing or hot isotactic pressing at 600–1400°C and 70–210 MPa for 1–4 h. [13, 14] Figure 3 summarizes the evolution of the structure from the powder state to the sintered material.

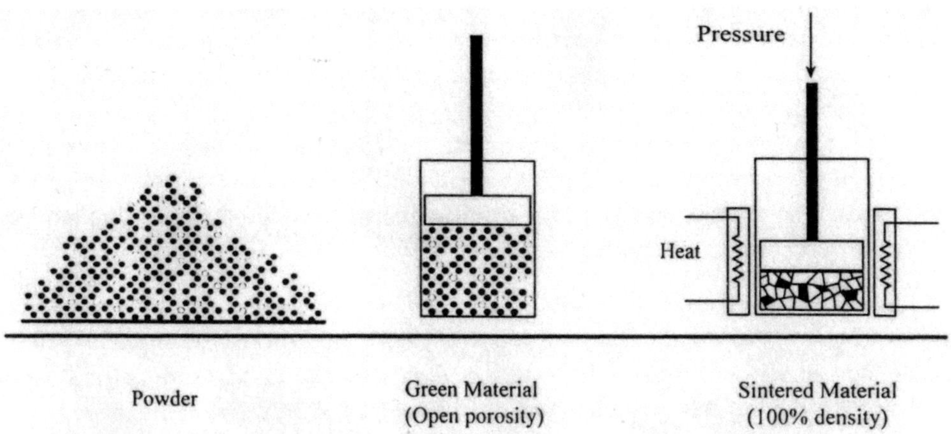

Figure 3. Consolidation process of nanophase powders.

Depending on the method of synthesis a variety of nanocomposites of the type shown in Figure 4 can be produced. [15] Nanocomposites are made by dispersing nanometer-scale particles of one material either inside the grains of a second material or between the grains. Combinations in which both phases are equally fine (nano–nano composites) are possible. The advantages of, for example, nanosize-reinforced metal–matrix composites include a combination of high strength, high elastic modulus, high toughness and impact properties, low sensitivity to temperature changes or thermal shock, high surface durability, and low sensitivity to flaws.

Defects that destroy the properties of the bulk nanophase material can nearly always be attributed to some specific event in the processing history. Strength-limiting effects can often be avoided if careful control is exercised over all aspects of processing, the most critical being the characteristics of the starting powder. The ideal characteristics of the starting powder for advanced materials are: [16]

http://dx.doi.org/10.5772/62024

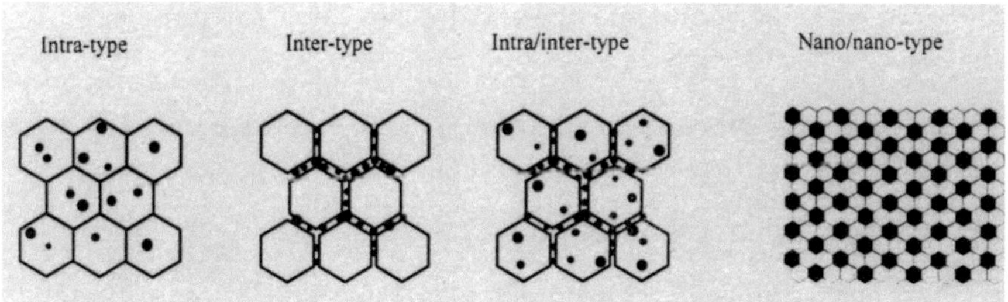

Figure 4. Types of nano-composites possible by nanophase material synthesis methods. [15]

- Spherical shape (to improve packing)
- Particle size below 100 mm in diameter
- A narrow size distribution (to improve packing, avoid grain growth and maximize grain – density)
- Freedom from agglomeration (to improve packing and minimize void fraction)
- Highly controlled purity

Contamination and the presence of hard agglomerates are the major limiting effects, and are probably the most difficult properties to control during the powder preparation process, as will be discussed in the next section. Highly controlled purity is important because the quality of the bulk nanophase material depends directly on the purity of the starting powders. However, nanophase materials usually are very susceptible to contamination. For example, tungsten in nanosize phase – in contrast to conventional tungsten – is highly pyrophoric.

Freedom from agglomeration is important to improve stability of the structure and to significantly reduce sintering time and temperature. Hard agglomerates must be avoided since their presence gives rise to the formation of pores and flaws during sintering. The pores slow down the sintering process, limit densification, and reduce the strength of the material by acting as crack formation sites. Hard agglomerates are distinguished from weak agglomerates by necking (bridging) that occurs between particles. This necking is due to surface reactivity, surface growth, or sintering. It is the hard agglomerate, not the weak agglomerate that is undesirable. For example, to produce optimum parts from fine ceramics particles, the powder must be compacted to low void fractions such that near-net-shape parts are obtained after sintering. The poor packing characteristics of hard agglomerates make them of little use to the ceramic industry. [17]

3. Powder preparation by aerosol processes

The methods shown in Table 2 have been used with different levels of success to produce ultrafine particles. Only gas-to-particle conversion processes are described here because of their widespread use and potential for large-scale production of materials. See References 18, 19, 20, and 21 for a general review.

Gas-to-particle conversion processes refer to production of particles from individual atoms or molecules in the gas phase. The processes constituting the overall process are well understood qualitatively and are shown in Figure 5. By using any high-energy source such as a flame, joule (resistive) heating, plasma, sputtering, ion, electron or laser beams, or a hot wall reactor, condensable product atoms or molecules are formed. Depending upon the kinetics, thermodynamics, reactor design, and operating conditions, the product atoms/molecules self-nucleate and form molecular clusters. Over a very short period of time, a high concentration of clusters is formed.

Production Methods of Nanosized Structures				
Method			Description	Characteristics
Mechanical grinding (Ball milling)			Repeated welding, fracturing, and rewelding of powders in a high-energy ball charge	Control of impurity content is difficult
Aerosol methods	Gas-to-particle	Flame reactor Furnace reactor Gas condensation Plasma reactor Laser ablation Sputtering	Evaporation of materials followed by condensation into ultrafine particles	Narrow size distribution, high purity, spherical and solid particles. Formation of hard agglomerates
	Spray pyrolysis			High purity. Appropriate for multicomponent materials Solubility problems can exist. Low production rates
	Film generation	Droplet deposition Chemical vapor deposition Solid participle deposition	Produces layered structures	
Solution phase methods			Reactants are diluted in an appropriate solvent, mixed together and particles are obtained by homogeneous precipitation	Extreme uniformity can be achieved. Applicable to limited range of compositions
Solid phase methods			Achieved by mixing the reactants powders together and heating of ignited to high temperatures	Starting materials may be synthesized in pure forms

Table 2. Production methods of nanosized structures.

The newly formed clusters grow by condensation of atoms/molecules or by coagulation with other clusters. Early in the process, particles possess very high surface energy. Therefore, the rate of particle sintering is extremely fast and colliding particles rapidly assume a spherical shape. As particles grow further, surface energy decreases substantially, the rate of particle sintering becomes slow and collisions among particles result in irregularly shaped particles (agglomerates). Figure 6 illustrates the typical agglomerated structures obtained.

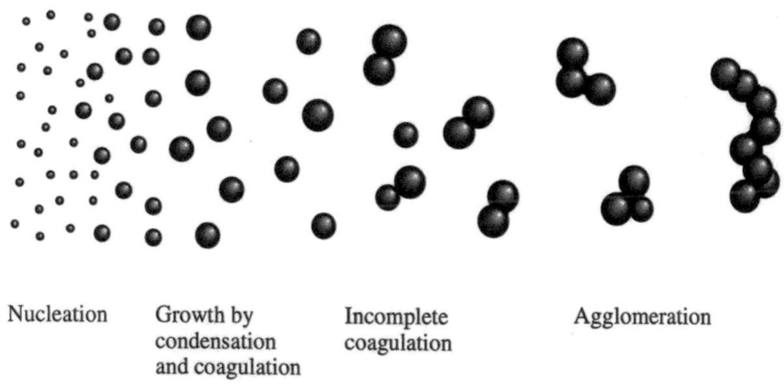

Figure 5. Processes occurring during powder production from aerosol processes.

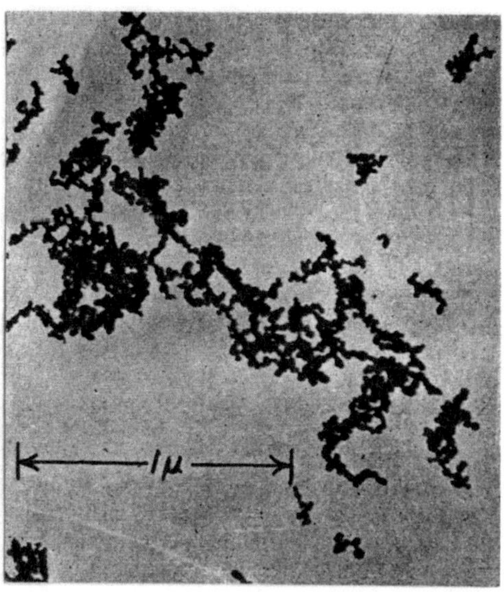

Figure 6. Long agglomerates formed during synthesis of nanosize tungsten by flame synthesis. [22]

The primary advantages of gas-to-particle routes are small particle size, narrow size distribution, nearby spherical solid particles, and high purity. The disadvantages for most aerosol methods include low production rates, chemical inhomogeneities for multicomponent materials, high energy costs, and problems associated with hazardous gaseous reactants and by-products. A critical disadvantage is the formation of hard agglomerates in the gas phase when number densities are high.

Unlike other aerosol processes, flames have high production rates and low energy costs, and the potential for scale-up is well established. [23] Figure 7 illustrates the process of particle formation by flame synthesis. Reactants are brought to a high temperature reactor either premixed or separately (nonpremixed) in a coflow configuration. When the reactants reach the flame front, reaction takes place. The products of the reaction process are the desired materials are often a gas-phase by-product. The desired material follows the gas-to-particle route described above, yielding nanosized particles. However, due to the high particle number densities and steep temperature gradients present during the entire process, hard agglomerates are usually formed, and flames traditionally offer poor control over particle size and morphology.

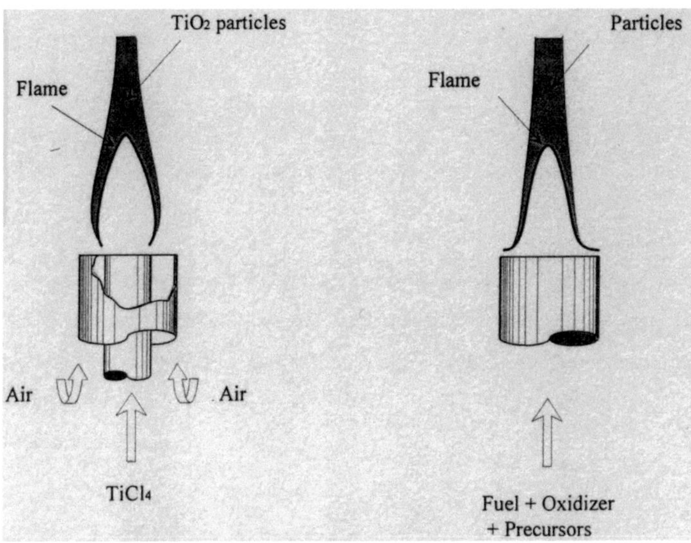

Figure 7. Illustration of the flame synthesis methods to produce nanosized materials.

4. Description of the problem

Some work has been performed to establish conditions to minimize agglomerate formation. Flagan and Wu [24] proposed controlling agglomeration in an aerosol reactor by maintaining a sufficiently low number concentration of primary nuclei and varying temperature along the reactor such that coagulation is minimized while condensation is maximized within the residence time of particles in the reactor. Zachariah and Dimitriou [25] noted that agglomerates are almost exclusively constructed from 10-30 nm primary particles and proposed controlling agglomeration by limiting the homogeneous nucleation rate in such a way that the 10-30 nm

http://dx.doi.org/10.5772/62024

primary particles can grow by heterogeneous condensation. Thus, they developed a set of criteria for determining the onset of runaway nucleation as the criteria to control agglomeration. These methods have not been demonstrated experimentally and are not applicable to high number density, high production rate methods of synthesis such as flame synthesis.

Recently, Axelbaum et al. [26] successfully demonstrated control of agglomeration inflames with a novel particle encapsulation approach. Figure 8 illustrates this process. The basic approach is to allow the nucleation and growth of the primary particles to proceed normally but then encapsulate these particles, with an appropriate material, when they have grown to the required size and before they begin to agglomerate, thus producing encapsulated particles. These particles will agglomerate, but the primary particle within them will not. When the encapsulation is later removed, the resulting powder will contain only weakly agglomerated particles. Encapsulation is accomplished by either encapsulating the particles with a byproduct of the combustion process or with an additive chosen for this purpose.

The encapsulation process is triggered to occur thermodynamically, kinetically or through mixing. The encapsulating material must be chosen such that it can be completely removed by, for example, heat treating or washing. Another important advantage of the encapsulation method is that it could protect air sensitive nanophase particles from oxidation or contamination during subsequent handling.

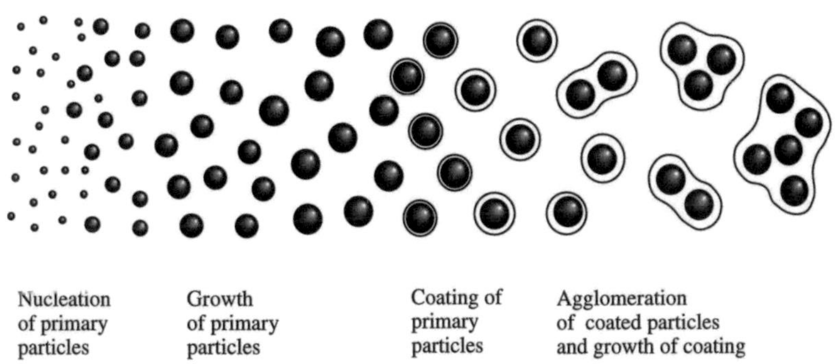

Figure 8. Illustration of the particle coating method to control agglomeration during gas-to-particle formation process.

5. Objectives

In previous sections it was stated that: 1) among the different methods of synthesizing nanosized powders, flame synthesis has by far the highest possible production rate, and it is the. only method in which scale-up to high production rates has been demonstrated, 2) hard agglomerates are usually formed during aerosol processes, particularly in flames, because of the high number densities and steep temperature gradients, 3) nanophase materials are very susceptible to contamination, 4) contamination and the presence of agglomerates destroys the properties of the nanophase bulk material, and 5) the encapsulation process could be an effective solution to control agglomeration, and to protect the primary particles from contamination.

The objectives of this work are to:

1. Demonstrate the applicability of the particle encapsulation method to the production of high purity, unagglomerated nano-particulates of tungsten (W) and tungsten titanium alloys (W-Ti) by flame synthesis.
2. Develop a Monte Carlo method to model particle dynamics in multi-component aerosols.
3. Apply the Monte Carlo method to study the processes occurring in two-component aerosols in order to understand the encapsulation process and evaluate approaches to optimize the encapsulation process as a solution to the particle contamination and agglomeration problems during the formation of nanosized powders in flames.

Specific objectives

In order to accomplish these objectives, several specific tasks must be performed:

- Apply the particle encapsulation methodology to produce high-purity, unagglomerated nanoparticles of W, Ti, and W-Ti by flame synthesis. This step requires:
    - Selecting the appropriate reactants for the production of W
    - Adapting the existing burner for the production of W
    - Producing ~20 g of nanosized W and W-Ti powder of optimal quality
    - Consolidating produced powder into bulk cylindrical pellets
- Identify and describe the variables and mechanisms controlling the encapsulation process.
- Formulate the mathematical equations that govern the physical processes occurring in flames and in multi-component aerosols. These processes include nucleation, condensation, and coagulation.
- Establish an appropriate methodology to solve the mathematical model in terms of the variables of interest: particle size distribution and composition.
- Validate the method of solution by comparing with analytical and experimental results available for simplified conditions.
- Apply the mathematical model to a simplified flame configuration, where the general equations reduce to their simplest form. The simplified configuration is equivalent to steady state systems where gas-phase precursors react in 1D flame.
- Describe the process of encapsulation under different conditions.
- Identify the conditions that will inhibit or promote effective encapsulation.
- Prescribe optimum operating conditions for the production of unagglomerated nanosized particles.

http://dx.doi.org/10.5772/62024

6. Outline

This document is organized in seven chapters with three appendices. Chapter 2 describes the production of high-purity, unagglomerated nanoparticulate of W, Ti, and W-Ti by flame synthesis. Chapter 3 contains the formulation of the model that describes the physical processes involved in multicomponent aerosols and the different methods that are available to solve the governing equations. Monte Carlo simulation is identified as the appropriate solution method for modeling multicomponent aerosol processes. Chapter 4 describes the Monte Carlo method developed to simulate coagulation. Chapter 5 describes the methodology used to model condensation processes and the coupling of coagulation and condensation. Chapter 6 provides a detailed description of the encapsulation process and explains the physics under which encapsulation occurs. Finally, Chapter 7 contains conclusions and recommendations for future work. Appendix A contains a heat transfer model to predict particle heating during condensation. Appendix B is a literature review about particle sintering, and Appendix C is a description of particle dynamics in colloidal systems.

Author details

Jose Ignacio Huertas

Address all correspondence to: jhuertas@itesm.mx

Tecnológico de Monterrey, Mexico

Section 2

Sodium/Halide Flame Synthesis of W and W-Ti Nanoparticles

Chapter 2

Sodium/Halide Flame Synthesis of W and W-Ti Nanoparticles

Jose Ignacio Huertas

Additional information is available at the end of the chapter

http://dx.doi.org/10.5772/62023

This chapter describes the experimental work employed to demonstrate the applicability of the particle encapsulation method to the production of high-purity unagglomerated nanosize tungsten (W), and tungsten titanium alloys (W-Ti) particles by flame synthesis. These materials possess unique properties that make them desirable for advanced applications. Some work has been carried out to produce ultrafine powders of W by flame synthesis. However, due to the high particle number densities and steep temperature gradients associated with flames, the produced W particles form long-chain agglomerates. Furthermore, pure W metal can be highly pyrophoric and an oxide contaminant is formed when the powder is exposed to atmosphere. Consequently, size, purity, and agglomeration are simultaneously the critical issues that need to be addressed in the synthesis of nanosized W.

This chapter begins by describing the existing needs for W and W-Ti nanoparticles. Subsequent sections describe the thermodynamics and experimental considerations for the synthesis of the powder. The chapter concludes by describing the experimental results obtained.

1. Need for nanosized W and W-Ti particles

Tungsten metal (W) and tungsten heavy alloys (WHA) possess unique properties that make them desirable for advanced applications. W has a very high density (19.3 g/cm3) and the highest melting point of all the elements (3410°C).

WHA are two-phase metal–matrix composites. Conventionally they are processed by premixing the W metal with binder elements such as Fe, Ni, Cu, or Co. The mixture is then compacted in either a mechanical, hydraulic, or isostatic press and consolidated by liquid phase sintering (LPS) in a protective atmosphere (hydrogen or vacuum) at a temperature where the minor constituents form a liquid. W content normally varies from 90 to 98 wt%. The final sintered microstructure consists of a contiguous network of nearly pure BCC W grains embedded in a ductile FCC matrix. The typical mean tungsten grain size varies from 30 to 60 μm. [27] WHA have a combination of high strength (800–1000 MPa), high ductility (10–30%), good electrical and thermal conductivity, corrosion resistance, and excellent machinability. [28]

Current applications for W and WHA include counterbalances in military aircraft, radiation shields, lighting components, ignition electrode materials, catalysts in the chemical industry, alloying elements for high speed steels, sputter targets in VLSI chip technology, and a variety of sport related parts. [29]

WHA are also being investigated as a replacement for depleted uranium (DU) alloys for kinetic energy penetrators (KEP) applications. Despite the excellent performance of DU alloys, replacements are being sought because of serious economical and political concerns associated with the significant health risk and decontamination cost associated with the manufacture and handling of DU. W and WHA are being pursued as alternatives [30, 28] because their densities are similar to DU alloys, and high density is the primary requirement for KEP. To date, the performance of WHA under high strain rate conditions has been inferior to DU, [27] and there is a great interest in developing WHA with improved KEP performance.

Much of the work both within the Army and in the commercial sector has been based on the premise that it is only necessary to improve the quasi-static mechanical properties of WHA in order to improve ballistic properties. Many metallurgical parameters have been investigated with regard to alloying elements, characteristics of the W starting powder, impurities, process parameter variations in the liquid phase sintering (LPS) cycle, post-sintering heat treatment, and matrix composition variations at constant W content. Although these studies have led to improvements in static properties, those improvements have not translated to improved high strain rate performance, [31] and the high strain rate properties are of critical importance for KEP applications.

DU penetration into semi-infinite targets has been shown to be characterized by localized (adiabatic) shear deformation that permits the penetrator to discard deformed material quickly along its flanks as penetration proceeds. This process leads to a "self-sharpening" effect that keeps the interface stress on the armor higher for a longer period of time. Such deformation contrasts with observations for WHA penetrators that deform by "mushrooming" at the nose, thereby spreading the impact force and lowering the interface stress and penetration distance. Figure 1 represents the deformation behavior of (a) a tungsten penetrator and (b) α Uranium alloy penetrator.

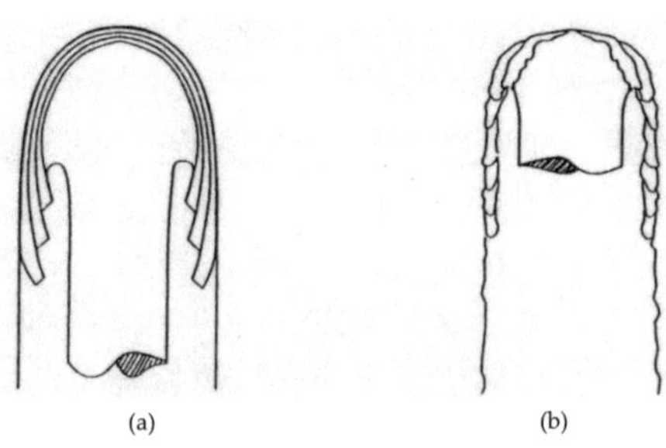

Figure 1. Representation of the deformation behavior of (a) a tungsten penetrator and (b) α Uranium alloy penetrator. [27]

It is believed that during high strain rate penetration, the WHA grains are heated under near adiabatic conditions, eventually passing through the ductile-to-brittle transition, and exhibiting flow softening at higher temperatures. [27] However, fracture events occur at the microstructural level at relatively small strains and before there has been significant heating. Cracks initiate at the W-W grain boundaries with as little as 3–5% plastic strain, and the matrix does not carry the load until ~30% plastic strain. Thus, there is a critical need to obtain control of the high strain rate penetrator performance of WHA by tailoring the initial composition and structure.

Penetration performance for WHA should be enhanced by improving room temperature plasticity at high strain rates. WHA with ultrafine grain sizes (<0.1 μm) may meet this requirement. Furthermore, low-temperature (<1500°C) densification can be enhanced during consolidation of ultrafine powders and ductility can be improved via the mechanism of grain boundary sliding. [32]

On the other hand, Magness et al. [27] have suggested replacing the ductile matrix in the WHA composite with one made of an alloy system that is more shear-prone, with a substantially lower softening temperature, to alleviate problems associated with high strain rate deformation in WHA. Metals that tend to display adiabatic shear tendencies are characterized by a low work-hardening rate, high thermal softening, and low strain rate sensitivity. In this regard, alloy systems such as titanium alloys have been recommended for matrix replacement. [27, 33]

Given the above motivation, a need exists for a W-Ti alloy with W content of 90–98 wt% and a microstructure consisting of ultrafine W grains embedded in a soft Ti matrix. The methodology proposed is to produce nanosized W, Ti, and W-Ti powders and then consolidate them at low temperature (~1000°C) to preserve grain size. Previous attempts to reach that objective have been unsuccessful because there has not been a reliable method availab1e to produce the ultrafine starting powders. [33]

Mechanical milling, [34] liquid phase synthesis, [35], [36] chemical vapor deposition (CVD), [37], [38] and gas-to particle conversion methods [22, 39, 40, 41] are possible sources of ultrafine W powders. Among these processes, flame synthesis has by far the highest possible production rates.

Production of ultrafine powders of W by flame synthesis started with Lamprey et al. [22] in 1962. In this work, an inverted coflow burner was employed to obtain submicron metal powder by hydrogen reduction of WCl_6. Future studies involved reacting tungsten halides in H_2/F_2 [40] or H_2/Cl_2 [41] flames. These approaches successfully produce W metal. Nonetheless, due to the high particle number densities and steep temperature gradients associated with flames, these processes offer poor control of particle size and morphology. Long-chain hard agglomerates were usually formed [22] (Figure l-6) and the pure metal W powders were often pyrophoric, or oxide contamination formed on exposure to atmosphere. [41]

2. Particle encapsulation to control agglomeration and oxygen impurities

The above problems are potentially avoided by using the particle encapsulation method developed by Axelbaum et al. [26], [42] and described in Section 4. Since W is produced through the reaction:

$$WCl_{6(g)} + 6Na_{(g)} \rightarrow W_{(s)} + 6NaCl_{(g)} \quad DH = -1241.3\ kJ/mole \tag{1}$$

the NaCl by-product was employed as the encapsulating material in these studies. NaCl is an effective encapsulating material because its boiling point is 1410°C, which allows condensation to be triggered in the flame by controlling temperature and NaCl concentration. The NaCl encapsulation can be removed by washing with an appropriate solvent or through vacuum sublimation at moderate temperatures (~800°C). Experimentally, the particle encapsulation process has been shown to be realizable; Ti, [42] TiB_2, [42] and AlN [43] particles encapsulated with NaCl have been obtained through the respective reactions:

$$TiCl_{4(g)} + 4Na_{(g)} \rightarrow Ti_{(s)} + 4NaCl_{(g)} \quad DH = -393.5\ kJ/mole \tag{2}$$

$$TiCl_{4(g)} + 2BCl_{3(g)} + 10Na_{(g)}\ TiB_{2(s)} + 10NaCl_{(g)} \tag{3}$$

$$AlCl_{3(g)} + NH_{3(g)} + 3Na_{(g)} \rightarrow AlN_{(s)} + 3NaCl_{(g)} + 1.5H_{2(g)} \tag{4}$$

Employing similar sodium-halide chemistry (Equation 1), the NaCl encapsulation process is well suited for the production of nanosized W and W-Ti because the salt by-product is produced in the reaction zone simultaneously with the core product particles. Sodium reduction of chlorides was first employed in the 1960s in the effort to produce high-purity silicon for semiconductors and solar cells through the reaction:

$$SiCl_{4(g)} + 4Na_{(g)} \rightarrow Si_{(s)} + 4NaCl_{(g)}{}^{44} \tag{5}$$

The main difficulty with this process is separating the silicon from the reaction by-product NaCl to yield solid silicon. Gould and Dickson [44] patented an impaction technique where the reaction products form a supersonic jet exiting from the reaction chamber. The jet impinges on a flat surface, whereupon the silicon particles deposit. Calcote and Felder [45] advanced this work, producing high-purity silicon, and proposed that many other materials, including Ti and W, could be produced by sodium/halide combustion synthesis. Glassman et al. [46] also proposed extending this chemistry to other materials, developed a thermodynamic criterion for selecting appropriate reactants, and employed Na/K-halide chemistry to produce TiN, TiB_2, TiC, $TiSi_2$, SiC, and B_4C. These authors, however, did not attempt to produce W or W-Ti, or unagglomerated nanosized particles.

Metals	Intermetallics	Ceramics
Si*		B_4C*
Mo		TiN*
W	$MoSi_2$	SiC*
Fe	TiAl	TiC*
Al	$TiSi_2$*	HfB_2
Ta	Ti_3Al	TaB_2
Zr	Ti_5Si_3	TaC
Nb		ZrB_2
Be		WC

*Materials produced via Na/K-halide combustion synthesis.

Table 1. Materials that can be produced by sodium-halide combustion synthesis. [45, 46]

3. Thermodynamic considerations

The relevant chemistry for synthesizing W and Ti is given in Equations 1 and 2. Chlorides of tungsten titanium react with sodium vapor to produce the parent metals and the by-product NaCl. Since the reaction of metal halides with sodium is known to be extremely fast, reaction considerations are dominated by thermodynamics.46 The NASA equilibrium code and commercial software were used to guide selection of operating conditions to obtain high yields of W and W-Ti. Thermodynamic yield is defined as the ratio of the moles of metal in the products per mole of metal chloride in the reactants.

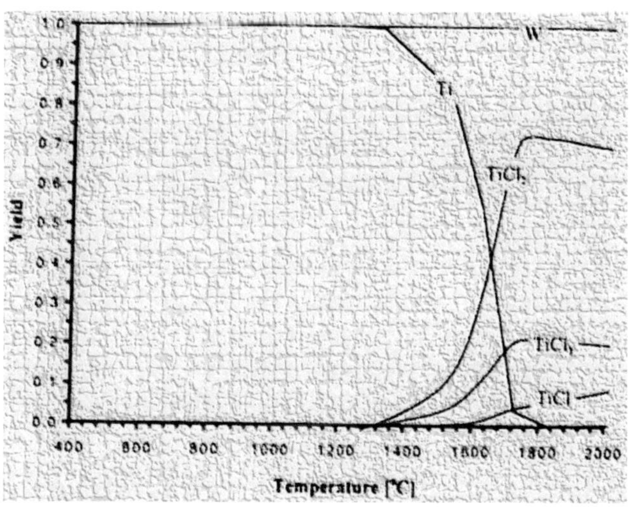

Figure 2. Equilibrium yields for the Ti/W/Cl/Na system.

Figure 2 shows the yield as a function of temperature for the W/Ti/Na/Cl system. The yield of Ti begins to drop rapidly at temperatures above ~1250 °C, yet the yield of W is 100% up to 2200°C. Various quantities of argon can be used in this process with little effect on thermodynamic yield. In a commercial system, argon can be readily recycled because at room temperature, the products are in condensed phases.

In comparison, thermodynamic calcu1ations for the W/H/C1 system, as employed in Reference 41, show that 100% yields can be obtained for tungsten, but only for temperatures below 1200°C. The reaction:

$$WCl_{6(g)} + 3H_{2(g)} \rightarrow W_{(s)} + 6HCl_{(g)} \qquad \Delta H = -60.1\ kJ/mole \tag{6}$$

is ~20 times less exothermic than Equation 1, and is thus less favorable. Furthermore, this system is not suitable for flame synthesis of Ti because the reaction:

$$TiCl_{4(g)} + 2H_2 \rightarrow Ti_{(s)} + 4HCl_{(g)} \qquad \Delta H = 393.9\ kJ/mole \tag{7}$$

is highly endothermic. The sodium/halide flame process can also be used to obtain W-Ti alloy or composite particles. The material can be produced *in situ* in a single, continuous operation. There are two ways to obtain the material: 1) by producing both metals at the reaction front:

$$TiCl_{4(g)} + xWCl_{6(g)} + (4+6x)Na_{(g)} \rightarrow xW - Ti_{(s)} + (4+6x)NaCl_{(g)} \tag{8}$$

or 2) by injecting the $TiCl_4$ downstream of the WCl_6, thus generating a new second reaction zone and producing Ti that will mix with and/or encapsulate the W. The first method is simpler but less flexible in terms of reinforcement size. In this study only the first method is considered.

4. The coflow sodium–halide burner

The coflow open atmosphere burner described in Axelbaum et al. [42, 43] is used in this study. The approach involves injection of the appropriate metal halide vapors into a laminar coflowing stream of sodium vapor. The burner consists of a set of heated concentric tubes with inner/outer diameters of 4/5, 11/13, 20/26, and 120/125 mm. Chlorides are supplied through the innermost tube, followed by Ar, then Na/Ar vapor, and finally Ar in the outermost tube. A detailed description of the burner can be found in References 42 and 43.

Tungsten chloride powder is heated in a quartz reservoir to 265°C (T_m = 275°C) yielding a saturation pressure of O.11 atm. Argon carrier gas is metered by a mass flow controller and is passed through the powder, and it is assumed that saturated conditions exist at the exit of the

http://dx.doi.org/10.5772/62023

reservoir. Liquid $TiCl_4$ heated in a stainless steel reservoir to 140°C (T_b = 136.4°C) and the flow rate of the vapor is metered with a high-temperature mass flow controller.

Sodium is heated to 150°C (Tm= 97.8°C) in a stainless steel reservoir. From there, it is pumped into the Na-vaporizer with a calibrated syringe pump. The Na-vaporizer consists of a porous cylinder wherein Ar carries Na vapor from the wetted walls. The temperature of the Na-vaporizer is fixed at 750°C where the saturation pressure of Na is 0.25 atm. Since liquid sodium at temperatures above 150°C will spontaneously ignite in air, the positive displacement syringe pump is employed to minimize the risk of uncontrolled release of liquid Sodium.

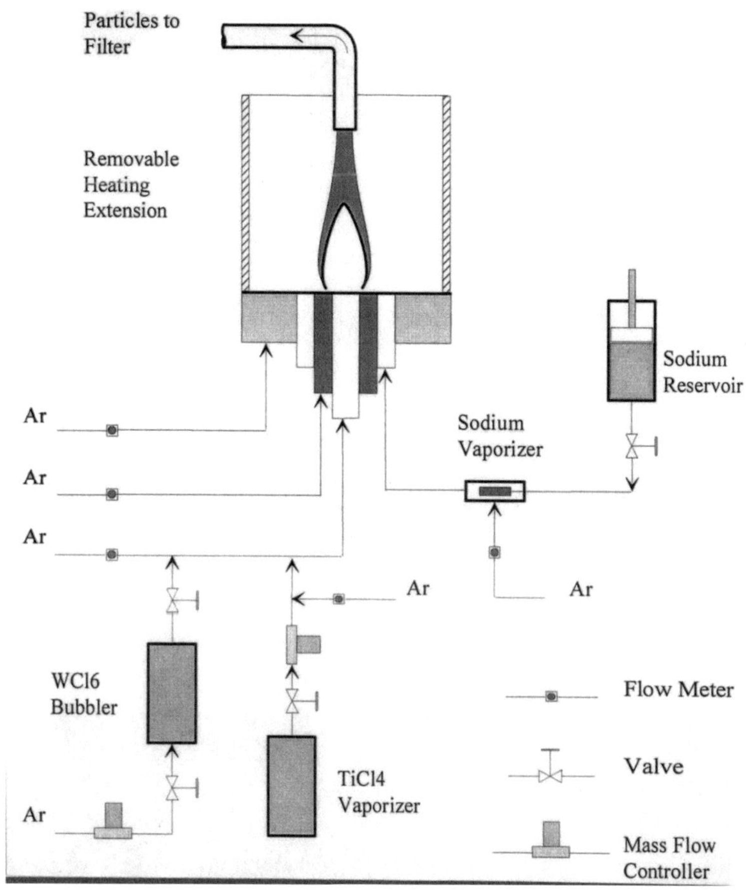

Figure 3. Burner schematic for production of W and W-Ti nanoparticles.

At the exit of the concentric tubes, reactants mix by diffusion and react spontaneously, producing a stable reaction zone. The reaction zone or flame appears as a bright yellow/orange zone having a shape similar to laminar hydrocarbon diffusion flames. Figure 4 shows a typical sodium/halide flame. Particles formed in the reaction zone are convected downstream, extracted by isokinetic sampling, and then collected onto a porous stainless steel filter.

Quantitative *in situ* laser measurements of particle size and number density have not been performed because the absorption spectrum of the sodium dimer in the visible spectrum is strong and broad. [47] Instead, an argon-ion laser is used to visually monitor scattering from particles to identify the particle-laden zones.

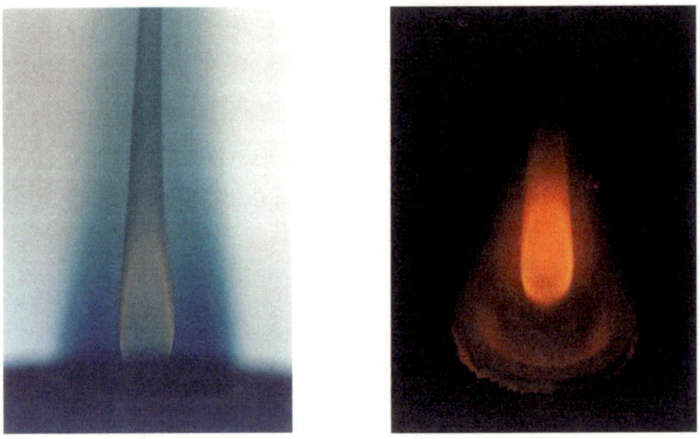

(a) (b)

Figure 4. Sodium flame for producing TiB2 nanoparticles: (a) backlit photograph (the purple/blue haze is due to light absorption by sodium vapor); (b) direct photograph from above. [42]

5. Synthesis of nanosized particles

Several runs were made to optimize the characteristics of the produced powder. The collected powders were characterized by X-ray diffraction (XRD), scanning electron microscopy (SEM), atransmission electron microscopy (TEM). XRD was used for phase identification of bulk powder samples and to obtain information about the size of the nanocrystallites using the X-ray line broadening method (i.e., the Scherrer formula). SEM and TEM studies of the powders were carried out to determine particle size distribution. Elemental composition was determined by energy disperse X-ray analysis (EDAX). Powders were exposed to atmosphere, and XRD characterization studies were performed in open atmosphere.

5.1. Production of nanosized W powders

Table 2 summarizes the various run conditions under which W powders were produced. XRD spectra of the as-produced powders show NaCl, α-W, and 5 extraneous peaks. After water washing, the salt is removed but the extraneous peaks remain (Figure 5). The extraneous peaks index reasonably well to either W_3O, W_3C, or β-W. However, β-W is a meta-stable phase that is known to stabilize to α-W [35, 36, 38] under heat treatment at temperatures greater than 450°C. Thus, the as-produced powder was heat treated under dynamic vacuum (-8×10^{-7} torr) at 800°C for 5 h. The extraneous peaks were no longer present, indicating that they were due to β-W. The remaining α-W peaks correspond to a particle size of 30 nm as determined by the Scherrer formula.

		Chlorine			Inner Shroud	Na		Outer Shroud
Run Number	T Burner °C	Flow SCCM	WCl_6 %	$TiCl_4$ %	Ar Flow SCCM	Flow SCCM	Na %	Ar Flow SLM
1	688	103	12		556	893	9	18.4
2	770	105	14		412	963	8	18.4
3	780	109	13		556	944	8	18.4
4	785	90	13		412	1405	15	18.4
5	640	145	4	1.0	1275	839	12	24.2
6	790	130	10	1.9	915	944	8	14.5
7	780	85	14	2.8	915	970	11	18.4
8	780	70	12	12.3	915	1229	13	18.4

Table 2. Run conditions for production of nanosized W (runs 1–4) and W-Ti (runs 5–8) powders.

For powders that were heat treated after exposure to atmosphere, XRD spectra show small peaks due to Na_2WO_4. Formation of Na_2WO_4 is due to the presence of Na in the as-produced sample. The Na is present because the flame is overventilated in Na, and thus, Na exists at the sampling location above the flame. The Na reacts with H_2O upon exposure to atmosphere, producing NaOH. During heat treatment, NaOH can react with W to produce Na_2WO_4 or $(Na_2WO_4)2H_2O$. Formation of these impurities is not an inherent concern since they can be eliminated by proper sampling and/or low temperature (~400°C) sublimation of the Na under dynamic vacuum. Indeed, XRD spectra for samples that were heat treated before being exposed to atmosphere do not show the Na_2WO_4 phase.

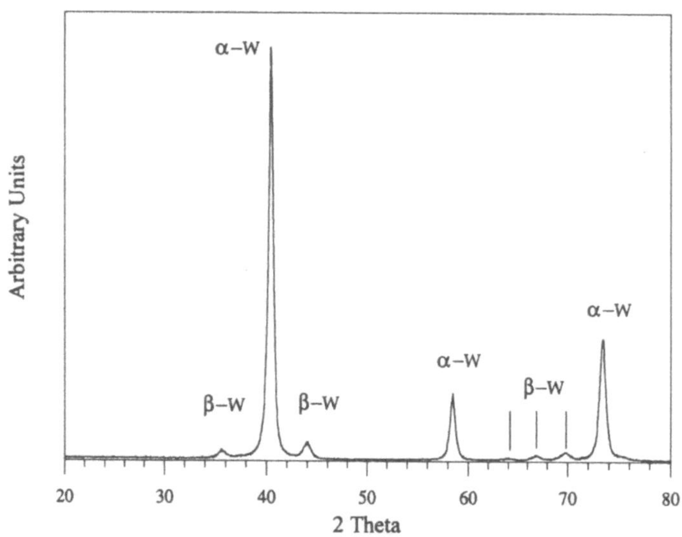

Figure 5. XRD of water-washed W sample for run No. 3.

Several batches of as-produced powder were water-washed with deionized, degassed water and dried under dynamic vacuum. A vigorous reaction was occasionally observed when the waterwashed powders were exposed to atmosphere. The sporadic pyrophoric nature of this ultrafine W is consistent with the findings for other flame-synthesized W. [22] On the other hand, the salt-encapsulated particles never reacted when exposed to atmosphere.

5.2. Production of nanosized W-Ti composites

The same configuration was used to produce nanosized W-Ti powders. Table 2 shows the run conditions. In all but run number 8, the flow rates of $WC1_6$ and $TiCl_4$ were set to obtain a ratio of 10 wt% Ti. Figure 6 shows the XRD spectra of the as-produced powders and reveals the presence of NaCl and α-W. No other phases are observed. The crystallite size of α-W determined by the Scherrer formula is ~30 nm. The XRD spectrum also does not show the presence of Ti. The Ti phase may be amorphous in the as-produced condition, or the amount of Ti may be insufficient to detect against the broad W background, or Ti may be in solid solution with W. When the powders are heat treated under dynamic vacuum (-lxl0^{-6} torr) at 850°C for 2 h, the salt is sublimed away and the XRD spectra of the heat treated samples show only broad peaks indexing to W (Figure 7). The particle size estimated by the Scherrer formula is ~40 nm, indicating that this heat-treatment does not increase the size of the W-Ti powders significantly. The sample is stable under atmospheric conditions and again there is no evidence of contamination or oxidation of the powders. The NaCl has also been removed by washing the powders with deionized, degassed water. The XRD results are similar to those obtained when the powder is heat treated.

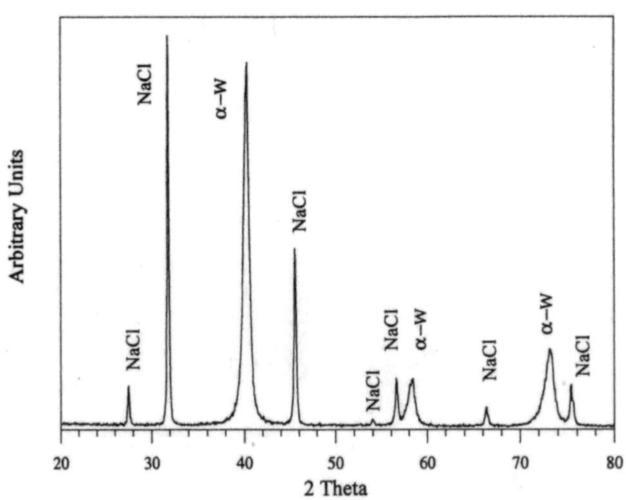

Figure 6. XRD of as-produced nanosized W-Ti for run No. 7.

SEM and TEM micrographs of the annealed W-Ti powders show particles of 40–50 nm in size. Figure 8 is a typical SEM micrograph, revealing that some of the particles are cubic while others

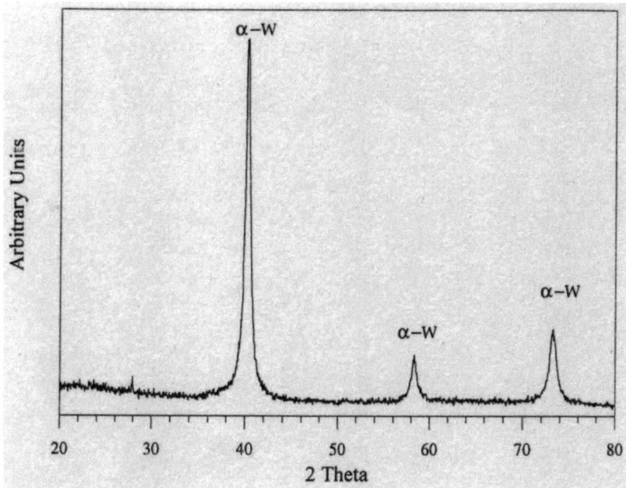

Figure 7. XRD of W-Ti sample for run No. 7, heat treated at 850°C for 8 h under dynamic vacuum.

are hexagonal. The micrograph also shows that particles are not in the form of long-chain agglomerates, but rather appear to be only loosely agglomerated. Figure 9 is a typical TEM micrograph of the as-produced particles, showing nanosized particles encapsulated in a NaCl matrix. Figure 8 together with Figure 9 show the effectiveness of the encapsulation process to control the presence of long-chain agglomerates.

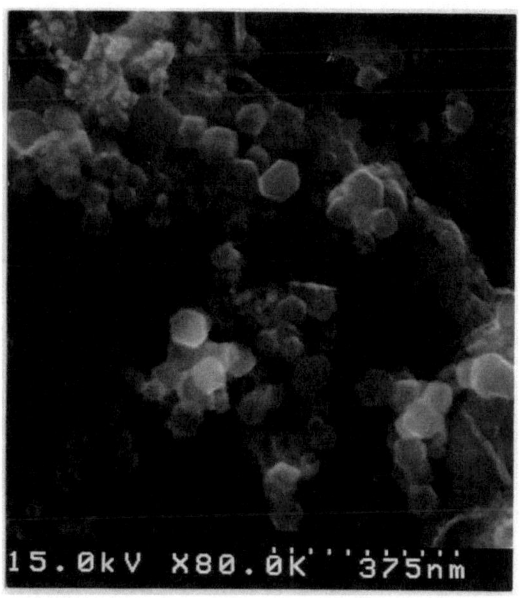

Figure 8. SEM micrograph of W-Ti sample for run No. 7, heat treated at 850°C for 2 h.

Figure 9. TEM micrograph of flame synthesized Ti particles of size ~75 nm encapsulated in NaCl.

Elemental analysis by ICP-atomic emission spectroscopy shows the presence of 15 wt% Ti. The fact that Ti is present, but not detected by XRD even after annealing, suggests that the Ti is in solid solution with W. Nonetheless, the equilibrium phase diagram of W-Ti [48] (Figure 10) shows that for this composition, Ti is also present as a separate phase, in addition to being in solid solution with W. To verify the presence of Ti as a separate phase, the effect of Ti addition on the lattice parameter was determined using XRD spectra. The experimental value of lattice parameter obtained using the XRD spectrum of the W-15 wt% Ti sample is 3.1680 x $10^{-[10]}$ m. The theoretical estimation of the lattice parameter of 15 wt% Ti in solution with W, calculated using literature values of lattice parameters for W(3.1653 x $10^{-[10]}$ m) and Ti (3.306 x $10^{-[10]}$ m), [49] and considering a linear variation of lattice parameter with alloying addition of Ti, gives 3.2500 x $10^{-[10]}$ m. This suggests that a substantial portion of the Ti is present as a separate phase.

To investigate the effectiveness of different methods of removing the NaCl from the as-produced samples, heat treated and water-wash samples were analyzed for Na and Cl (NSL Analytical Services, Inc.). Na was determined by ICP mass spectroscopy and Cl by ion chromatography. Table 3 shows the results. These tests indicate that the salt encapsulation of the particles may be effectively removed. Similar elemental analysis tests have shown the effectiveness of the NaCl encapsulation method protecting the powder from contamination

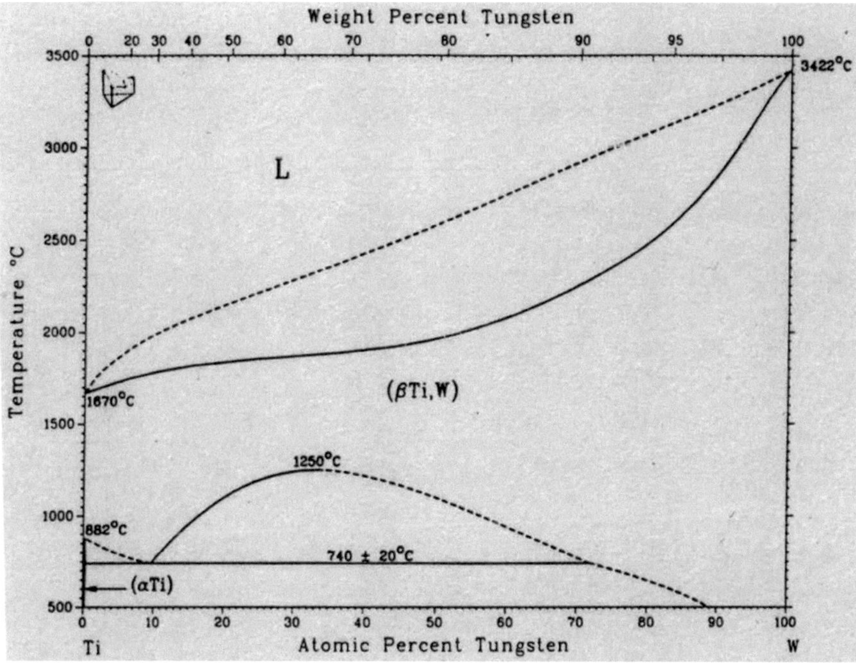

Figure 10. Equilibrium phase diagram for W and Ti. [48]

[43] In Reference 43, nanosized AlN was synthesized with an 0_2 content <0.8 wt%, while traditional methods offer AIN with an 0_2 content >5 wt%.

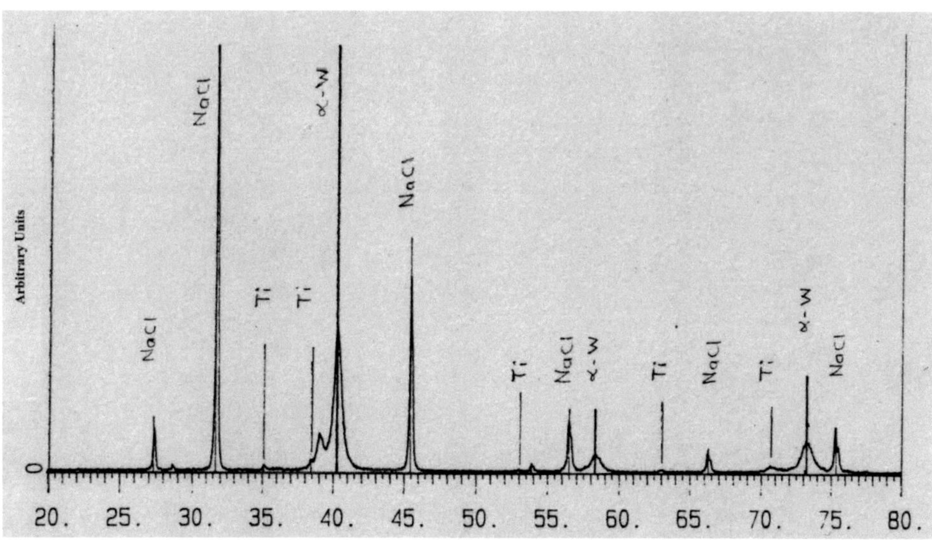

Figure 11. XRD of W-Ti sample for run No. 8.

Sample ID	Sal removal method	Residual by wt%	
		Na	Cl
W-Ti for run No 7	HT at 850°C for 10 h	0.025	0.02
W-Ti for run No 8	Water-washed	0.82	0.18

Table 3. Residual Na and Cl after salt removal of W-Ti samples as determined by elemental analysis.

In run number 8, the flow conditions were set to yield a composition of 78 wt% W and 22 wt % Ti. In this case, the XRD spectra of the as-produced sample reveals the presence of W, NaCl, and small peaks indexing to α-Ti and β-Ti (Figure 11).

6. Consolidation of W and W-Ti nanoparticles

As-produced powders were either water-washed or vacuum-annealed at 850°C, 10^{-6} torr for 2 h to sublime the protective NaCl encapsulation. The heat treatment setup used for vacuum-annealing the powders was transferred into an argon glove box for hot pressing. This procedure eliminated exposure of annealed powders to air. The nanosized W and W-Ti powders were consolidated into pellets of 6 mm diameter and 6–8 mm long.

The powders were pressed in a hot press located within the argon glove box. The hot press (Figure 12) consists of a furnace with molybdenum heating elements capable of reaching a maximum temperature of 1600°C. The hydraulic press is equipped to generate a maximum load of 225 KN.

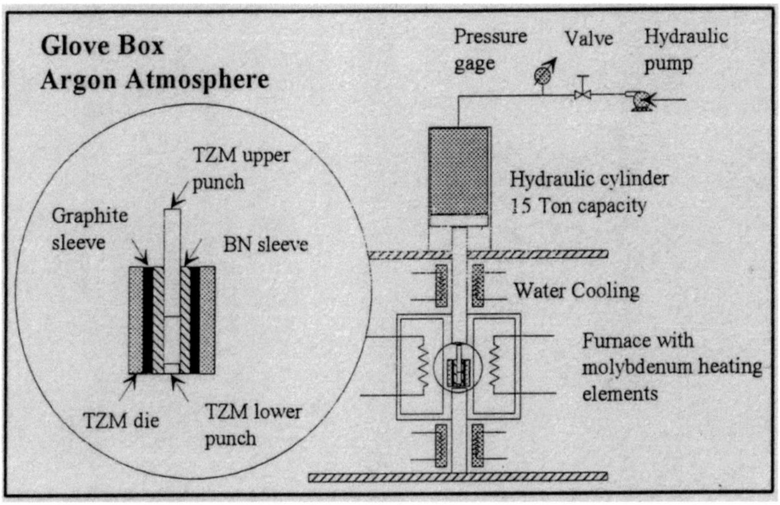

Figure 12. Hot press for consolidation of W and W-Ti particles.

http://dx.doi.org/10.5772/62023

The dies and punches used in hot pressing were made of TZM alloy (a molybdenum alloy), which has excellent high-temperature strength and oxidation resistance. A composite sleeve consisting of boron nitride (BN) and graphite was fitted into the TZM die. The inner BN sleeve minimized contamination of the W and W-Ti powders with carbon, while the outer graphite sleeve facilitated easy removal of the sample after consolidation.

The nanosized W-Ti powders were cold pressed by applying pressures up to 70 MPa. The hot pressing of the powders was carried out at 1000°C and 1200°C at a pressure of 175 MPa for 2–3 h. Table 4 summarizes the hot pressing conditions for consolidation of the W-Ti powders. After hot pressing, the consolidates were cooled slowly to room temperature and the pellets were removed from the TZM die and punch assembly. W-Ti consolidates were characterized using XRD, SEM, and TEM. The extent of densification indices were obtained by comparing the density of the consolidates to theoretical density values. Densities were measured by Archimedes principle and by measuring the dimensions of the cylindrical consolidates.

Sample	Hot Pressing Conditions			Results	
	T	P	Time	Densification	VHN
	°C	MPa	H	%	
W-13 wt% Ti No 1	1200	172	2	96	850
W-13 wt% Ti No 2	1200	172	3.5	97	800
Conventional W	N/A	N/A	N/A	100	295

Table 4. Hot pressing conditions for consolidation of the W and W-Ti powders.

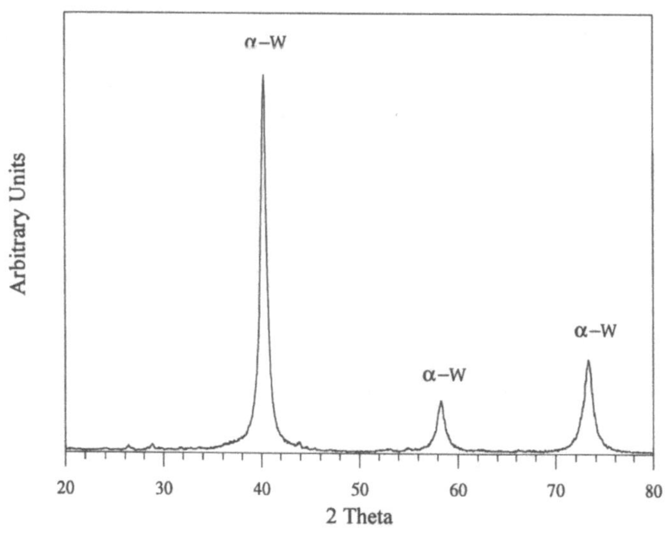

Figure 13. XRD of W-13 wt% Ti consolidated No. 2.

Figure 13 shows the XRD spectra of the W-Ti consolidate obtained under conditions No. 2. It shows broad peaks indexing to W. Figure 14 shows the SEM micrograph of the same W-Ti consolidate. As seen from the figure, the grain size of the consolidate is about 40 nm. The EDAX analysis, performed in conjunction with the SEM, shows 87 wt% W and 13% Ti. Figure 15 shows an optical micrograph of the consolidate No. 2, etched by Kcroll's reagent to show the Ti grains in the matrix. This figure shows the uniformity in the structure of the consolidate.

Though the temperatures maintained for hot pressing were between $0.36T_m$ and $0.40T_m$, the densification achieved after hot pressing was very high (~97%). Conventional materials can be consolidated to high density only by hot pressing at temperatures above ~$0.5T_m$. This shows that for WHA alloys, which possess very high melting temperatures, consolidation of nano-sized powders at relatively low temperatures into high density compacts is a viable and attractive route. Table 4 shows hardness values for nanocrystalline W and W-Ti consolidates as compared with conventional W. The hardness values are very high, as high as 4 times that of conventional W.

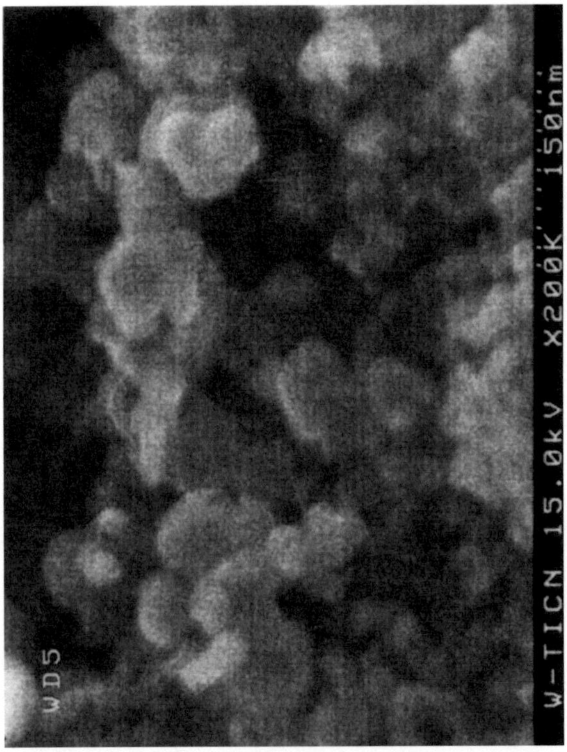

Figure 14. SEM micrograph of the W-13 wt% Ti consolidate No. 2.

The consolidated samples were hot isostatic pressed (hipped) to obtain 100% densification. Work is underway to test the mechanical properties of the fully dense consolidates under high strain rate conditions.

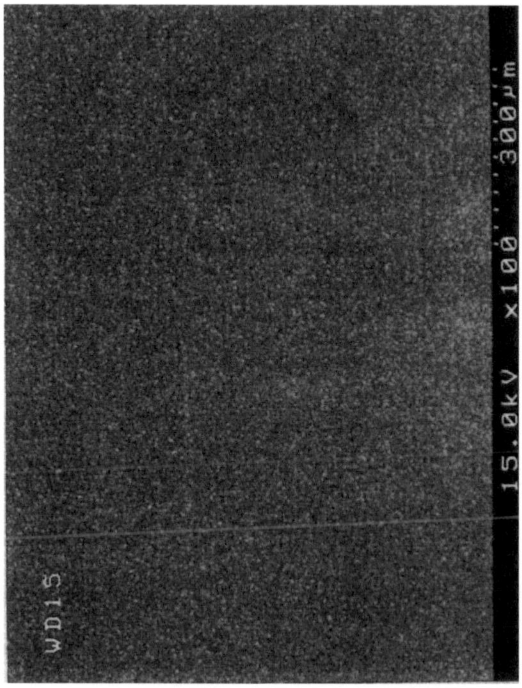

Figure 15. Optical micrograph of the W-13 wt%Ti consolidate No. 2. Etched by Kcroll's reagent to show the Ti grains in the matrix.

7. Summary

High-quality nanosized W and W-Ti nanoparticles have been produced, characterized, and consolidated to demonstrate the applicability of the sodium/halide flame synthesis and particle encapsulation process.

Nanocrystalline W particles were produced by reacting Na and WCl_6 and were characterized by XRD, SEM, TEM, and EDAX. The W particles appear unagglomerated, cubic and hexagonal in shape, and have an average size of ca. 30 nm. XRD results indicate the presence of only α-W, β-W, and NaCl. No contamination was detected even after extended exposure to atmospheric conditions. Vacuum heat treatment of the powders at 800°C results in effective removal of NaCl with no detectable change in particle size.

A powder consisting of nanosized W-Ti was also produced via $Na/WCl_6/TiC_4$ chemistry. XRD spectra of as-produced powders show only W and NaCl. EDAX indicates the presence of Ti, and analysis of lattice parameters suggests that part, not all, of the Ti is in solid solution. Particles are unagglomerated, cubic in shape, with an average size of ca. 30 nm. Heat treating the sample at 850°C increases average particle size to ca. 40 nm. When the amount of Ti is increased to 22 wt%, XRD spectra of as-produced powders show small peaks of α-Ti and β-Ti, in addition to W and NaCl. The nanosized W and W-Ti powders were successfully consolidated into pellets of 6-mm diameter and 6–8-mm long. Densities as high as 97% were achieved by hot pressing at temperatures of $0.42T_m$ to $0.48T_m$. Microstructures of the consolidates consist of nanometer-sized grains (40 nm). Hardness measurements indicate hardness values 4 times that of conventional tungsten. A 100% densification was achieved by hipping the samples. Work is underway to test the mechanical properties of the fully dense consolidates under high strain rate conditions.

The improvement in mechanical properties of the materials produced by flame synthesis, and the experimental results showing the effectiveness of the encapsulation method to control agglomeration and purity warrant further investigation. Consequently, the following chapters are devoted to studying particle formation and encapsulation processes in two-component aerosols. A mathematical model that describes the dynamics of the aerosol will be developed and the solution of that model will provide a description of the evolution of the particles, the dominant variables controlling the processes, and the desired methodology to optimize the encapsulation process.

Author details

Jose Ignacio Huertas

Address all correspondence to: jhuertas@itesm.mx

Tecnológico de Monterrey, Mexico

Section 3

Modeling Aerosol Processes

Chapter 3

Modeling Aerosol Processes

Jose Ignacio Huertas

Additional information is available at the end of the chapter

http://dx.doi.org/10.5772/62021

The term aerosol refers to an ensemble of liquid or solid particles suspended in a gaseous medium. The study of aerosols is relevant to a variety of fields, including air pollution, combustion, and chemical engineering. Since the 1950s, advances in aerosol science have been driven by investigations into the health effects of radioactive aerosols and industrial aerosols in the workplace and the environment. More recently, much effort has gone into understanding the effect of various natural and anthropomorphic aerosols on global warming. These efforts have largely been aimed at reducing the adverse effects of aerosol particles.

On the other hand, a great deal of knowledge has been recently gained by researchers working with *desirable anthropomorphic aerosols* used to produce nanophase high-technology materials such as ceramic powders, superconducting materials, and optical fibers. In this regard, aerosol processes are commercially employed for large-scale production of particle commodities like carbon black and inorganic powders (titania, zinc oxide, and fumed silica) and high-purity materials (optical fibers, thin films for micro-electronics, and advanced ceramics). The annual U.S. production amounts to hundreds of millions of tons. [23]

1. The General Dynamic Equation (GDE) for single-component aerosols

To understand the detailed behavior of aerosol systems, it is necessary to model the dynamic behavior of the aerosol population. Several mathematical models have been developed to simulate the physical processes that affect aerosols. Such processes include nucleation, coagulation, growth due to condensation of gases, shrinkage due to evaporation, sedimentation, and deposition on surfaces. Assuming that a particle in the aerosol can be described by a variable υ to represent its size (e.g., mass, vo1ume, or diameter), the general dynamic equation (GDE) that describes the behavior of a single component aerosol is: [50]

$$\frac{\partial n}{\partial t}+\nabla\cdot Vn=\nabla\cdot D\nabla n+\left(\frac{\partial n}{\partial t}\right)_{growth}+\left(\frac{\partial n}{\partial t}\right)_{coagul}+S_o\delta\left(\upsilon-\upsilon^*\right)-R \tag{1}$$

where n(υ,χ,t)dυ is the continuous distribution function that specifies the concentration of particles in the size range [υ, υ+dυ] at position x and time t. This equation is obtained through a material balance on a control volume fixed in space with respect to laboratory coordinates. The convective term ($\nabla \cdot Vn$) gives the change in the distribution function due to the bulk flow of the aerosol. The diffusion term ($\nabla \cdot D\nabla n$) accounts for changes in n due to gradients in particle concentrations. R represents the removal processes such as sedimentation or deposition on surfaces. $S_0\delta(\upsilon-\upsilon^*)$ represents the rate of generation of new particles where δ is the delta function. New particles may be generated by homogeneous nucleation, or any other mechanism. For example, a chemical reaction front or a combustion flame can be treated as sources of clusters, particles, and/or gas-phase products.

These four terms represent processes that may be called external since they involve movement across the walls of an elemental volume. However, particles in a given size range may also be modified as a result of internal processes such as growth and coagulation. The growth term in Equation (1) describes the rate of change of the distribution function n due to particle growth by condensation of the vapor phase material. The coagu1ation term describes the changes in the distribution function due to coalescing collisions between particles. In Chapters 4 and 5 we will present expressions for the coagulation and the condensation term, respectively.

2. Multicomponent aerosols

Even though common aerosols, e.g., atmospheric aerosols, are made of several species rather thana single one, little work has been reported on modeling the evolution of multicomponent to model the particle encapsulation process, and the GDE needs to be generalized to account for processes involving several species. To do so, a new variable **Y** is introduced to represent composition. **Y** is a p-dimensional vector where the Y_i represents the mass fraction of the ith species present in the particle, and p is the total number of species present in the aerosol. Y_i is given by:

$$Y_i = \frac{\textit{Mass of species i present in the particle}}{\textit{Total particle mass}}$$

such that $O < Y_i < 1$, and $\Sigma\, Y_i = 1$. Now, Equation (1) is the appropriate equation for modeling the particle dynamics with n(υ,**Y**,x,t)dυd**Y** being the continuous distribution function that specifies the concentration of particles in the size range [υ,υ+dυ] with composition in the range [**Y**, **Y**+d**Y**] at position **x** and time t in the aerosol.

In general, particles of the same size may have different chemical composition and the composition of a particle affects its growth rate. Thus, the computation of size distribution should generally not be performed independent of particle composition. Despite this, it is reasonable to assume that the rate of collision depends only on the sizes of the particles involved and not on their composition. Consequently, the usual expressions for coagulation, diffusion coefficient D, and collision frequency function β can be used. This also implies that interactions such as attractive or repulsive forces developed between particles of different materials are not considered.

Similarly to the case of single component aerosols, the dynamics of particle collisions is reduced to the assumption that the particles stick together with a probability α, which is known as the accommodation or sticking coefficient. For simplicity, α is assumed to be equal to 1. In addition, it is assumed that no chemical reaction occurs among the components in the particles. Consequently, when a collision between a particle of mass υ_i and composition Y_i with another particle of mass υ_j and composition Y_j occurs, a new particle of mass $(\upsilon_i + \upsilon_j)$ and composition $Y_k = (Yi^*\upsilon_i + \upsilon_j^*Y_j)/(\upsilon_i + \upsilon_j)$ is formed.

3. Solution methods

From a mathematical point of view, the modeling of multicomponent aerosols and the particle encapsulation process reduces to solving the GDE under the assumptions described in previous sections. The GDE, being a nonlinear integro-differential equation, will be solved numerically. To reach the objectives of this dissertation, the numerical method chosen must:Model coagulation and condensationTreat multicomponent aerosolsInclude the Kelvin effect, particle heating due to condensation, and heat loss from the aerosol

3.1. Solution method for single-component aerosol

Several works have been conducted to solve the GDE. Much of the effort to solve this equation has involved conditions where only coagulation is important. This information is of particular importance because the nonlinearity of the GDE comes from the coagulation term. Reference 58, which is a comparative review of mathematical models for aerosol dynamics, considers four approaches to the solution of the GDE. They are classified according to their representation of the size distribution and differ only in their degree of approximation of the size distribution.

- Continuous representation (e.g., J-Space method [51])
- Parameterized representation (e.g., Similarity solution [52])
- Discrete representation (e.g., Sectional method [54])
- Probabilistic methods (e.g., Monte Carlo method [55])

Those techniques that offer any desired degree of approximation are referred to as *continuous.* A typical example is the method known as the J-Space method. [51] This method is based on the use of the transformation $m(J) = m(J_o)^*Exp\{ \alpha^*(J-J_o) \}$, where m is mass, J and J_o are positive integers such that $J \geq J_o$ and α is an adjustable parameter. The coagulation equation is expressed in terms of this transformation, resulting in a set of integro-differential equations, one for each value of J. The set of equations are solved through the cubic spline interpolation method. The method is useful for numerical solution of continuous distributions over a wide particle size range; however, it has inherent problems associated with mass conservation and numerical dispersion. Numerical dispersion appears as waves ahead of or behind regions of high concentration.

Parameterized representations are those methods in which the size distribution is assumed to adhere to a known "self-preserving" form described by a small number of parameters. Solutions found in this way are believed to be asymptotic forms approached after long times. The assumption reduces the problem to solve a set of few ODEs for the parameters representing the distribution function. Within this category is the well known *method of moments.* Here the distribution function is assumed to be lognormal, and the governing equations are solved in terms of the first 3 moments of the size distribution function, representing the total number of particles, mean size, and dispersion of the distribution, respectively. [53] This method is simple but not suitable to model condensation because when condensation occurs, it cannot be assumed that the particle size distribution adheres to a specific distribution function.

In *discrete* representation methods, the size distribution is divided into a discrete number of sections (m), within which all the particles are assumed to be of the same size. Even though this approach is more complex than other methods, it is very popular due to its generality. The *sectional method* [54] falls into this category. In it, the solution is obtained in terms of the first moment for each section $n_i =) n(\upsilon)d\upsilon$. n_i represents the total number of particles per unit volume within section *i.* The overall rate of change of n_i is reduced to a set of *m* (the number of sections) ordinary differential equations by deriving expressions for the net rates by which particles are (i) added to section *i,* (ii) removed from section *i,* and (iii) remain in section *i.* The degree of approximation of this technique is limited by the number of sections used, i.e., to the maximum number of ODEs that can be solved simultaneously.

The *Monte Carlo* techniques are methods of statistical sampling of events to determine the average behavior of a system. They have been applied to simulate coagulation [55] and agglomeration. [56] The convenience, ease, directness, and expressiveness of the method makes them an attractive alternative; however, they require large amounts of computational time and memory that until recently has been computationally prohibitive.

3.2. Solution methods for multicomponent aerosols

Due to the diversity of techniques for computing size distribution dynamics of single-component systems, one approach to the multicomponent problem is to use a single variable, such as the mass of one of the components in the particle, to characterize the particle size and composition. Assuming that the characteristic component is conserved during coagulation, the masses of the nonconserved components in the particle may be determined by an auxiliary constraint, typically thermodynamic equilibrium. Such an approach has been reported for H_2SO_4-H_2O aerosols. [57] In this case it is assumed that H_2SO_4 is the characteristic component that is conserved by coagulation, and the water content of the particle is determined by thermodynamic equilibrium. Therefore, only the distribution of H_2SO_4 with time needs to be determined. Although an attractive feature of the approach is the reduction of the size of the problem, it is greatly limited to systems for which auxiliary constraints are valid and can be obtained.

In a more general approach, the techniques for single-component aerosols have been extended to include condensation/evaporation of the same or of a second material. Only the sectional method has been considered because the fundamental assumptions of the continuous and parameterized representation approaches are not valid when condensation occurs. Gelbard and Seinfelds[8] extended the sectional method to account for composition in multicomponent aerosols. They assumed that all the particles within a section have a constant size and composition and that coagulation and condensation are independent of particle composition. Then the governing equations are reduced to a set of m x z ODEs, where m is the number of sections for the size range and z the number of species (components) present in the aerosol. Therefore, this approach neglects that particles of the same size could have different compositions.

At high rates of condensation, three main problems appear [59]: the first is numerical diffusion. This problem arises because growth by condensation is a hyperbolic differential equation. Numerical diffusion lowers the peak value and broadens the size distribution, as shown in Figure 1. The second problem is conservation of mass of both gas-phase and particles during growth. Often, growth models subtract off the amount of gas removed by aerosol growth. However, subtracting can result in negative gas concentrations, requiring subsequent adjustments. The third problem is associated with the wide range of timescales for aerosol processes. Since the particle size domain may extend over several orders of magnitude in particle diameter, the characteristic timescales for particle growth may also have large variations. This results in stiff systems of differential equations. Such systems require special solution techniques that are not robust and are computationally expensive. [61]

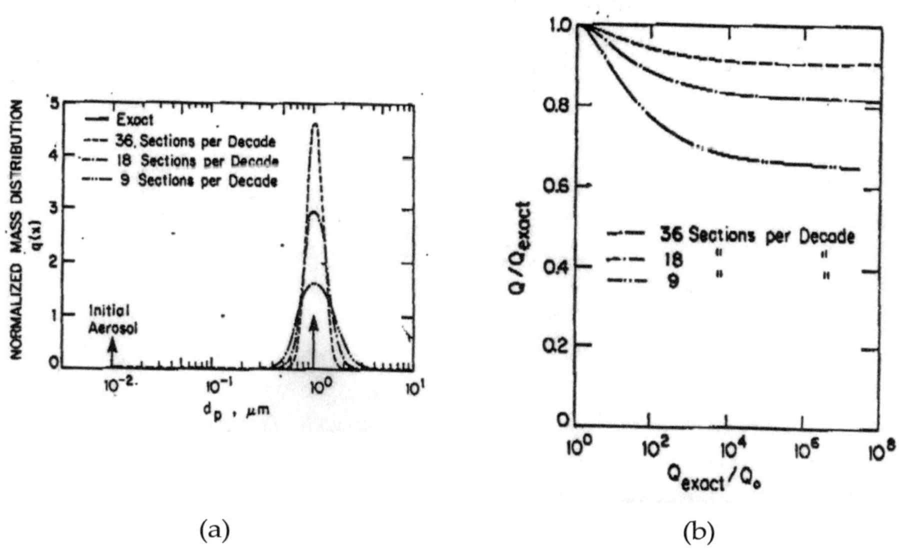

Figure 1. (a) Condensation growth showing normalized sectional mass distributions for a monodisperse aerosol whose diameter has increased 100-fold. (b) Deviation of sectional aerosol mass from the analytical solution with time. Q is the total mass in the section and q(x) is the total mass in the section divided by the length of the section. (From Reference 60)

The sectional method creates numerical diffusion because when mass moves to larger (condensation) or smaller (evaporation) sections, it distributes itself uniformly throughout the section. As a result, the distributed mass can quickly grow or evaporate to the next larger or smaller section the very next time step. This error can be reduced by drastically refining discretization. However, the computational effort for such approach is prohibitive. Quadrupling the number of sections that span the size range will halve the numerical diffusion. [60] By studying the resulting linear differential equations for a constant condensable vapor concentration, Gelbard [61] showed that the fixed-grid approaches cannot overcome numerical diffusion. Applying the *particle ordering principle,* and using a moving grid, the issue was resolved for situations when only condensation or evaporation is important. The particle ordering principle states than when particles grow or shrink by condensation or evaporation, respectively, particles of the same initial size will always preserve their respective ordering in particle size distribution. Consequently, the boundaries of a moving section will never cross. Unfortunately, the particle ordering principle may not be preserved in multicomponent aerosols. For example, in a condensing environment, small hygroscopic particles may surpass in size initially larger but insoluble particles. Furthermore, the moving grid method cannot be used when there is simultaneous condensation and coagulation.

Jacobson and Turco [62] advanced this idea and developed a model that uses a hybrid size grid. They used a moving size grid for condensation/evaporation and a stationary grid for other processes, such as coagulation, and nucleation. With this model, particles are assumed to be composed of an involatile core and a coating of a second condensable phase. The assumption of same size and composition for all particles within a grid still remains. Initially, the size distribution is organized within the sections in order of increasing core mass as opposed to increasing total mass. When coagulation among uncoated cores occurs, the mass of the new formed core is distributed evenly among the sections having cores with masses immediately larger and smaller than the new formed core. For example, if sections A, B, C, and D contain particles with cores of masses 2, 4, 8, and 16 units, respectively, coagulation among particles coming from sections B and C will result in a core of mass 12 units. Then half of the mass of the particle is added to section C and the other half to section D. Consequently, the number of particles in section B is reduced by one, section C is reduced by half, and section D increased by half. On the other hand, the moving grid contains the total mass of the particles (core plus coating). Then, during condensation or evaporation, particles are not transferred between sections; instead, their total masses increase or decrease to their exact sizes. To simulate coagulation among coated cores, it is assumed that when two coated cores combine, they form a third particle of a composition that falls between the characteristic compositions of two adjacent sections, i.e., the methodology for uncoated cores is applied regardless of the composition of the new formed particle. Clearly, this leads to problems in the conservation of mass of the condensable phase.

In summary, it has been shown that the coagulation equation must be solved through numerical methods. Among the many techniques available, the sectional method, although is not the simplest, is well accepted due to its generality. Contrary to the case of coagulation, there is a general analytical solution for the condensation equation, [63] but the numerical

http://dx.doi.org/10.5772/62021

techniques available for its solution possess several inherent problems like numerical dispersion, numerical diffusion, and an inability to conserve mass of the components. Only with a moving-grid-type technique can a proper numerical solution be obtained. However, this technique is not compatible or applicable when there is simultaneous coagulation and condensation.

Then there exists a need for a robust numerical technique to solve for coagulation and condensation simultaneously. In addition, the technique should be able to handle multicomponent aerosols with no restrictions in particle size and composition.

4. The solution method proposed

In the process of selecting the most convenient numerical technique to simultaneously solve the coagulation and condensation equation to study the encapsulation process, it was found that the Monte Carlo method possesses several advantages that make it an attractive route:

- The Monte Carlo method is intrinsically compatible with probabilistic phenomena like the coagulation process.
- The Monte Carlo method can be coupled to other probabilistic and deterministic approaches.
- The rate of particle growth is a simple ODE that can be solved very easily in a deterministic manner.

The proposed methodology is to simulate coagulation with the Monte Carlo method and couple it through time to a deterministic solution of the condensational growth equation. The coupling is obtained by using the time step for coagulation as the time step for condensation. The following chapter describes the Monte Carlo method adopted. Chapter 5 describes the solution of the equations for particle growth by condensation and the methodology used to couple the two solutions.

Author details

Jose Ignacio Huertas

Address all correspondence to: jhuertas@itesm.mx

Tecnológico de Monterrey, Mexico

Section 4

Monte Carlo Simulation of Coagulating Aerosols

Chapter 4

Monte Carlo Simulation of Coagulating Aerosols

Jose Ignacio Huertas

Additional information is available at the end of the chapter

http://dx.doi.org/10.5772/62021

Coagulation describes the process by which particles that are suspended in a fluid come into contact and coalesce or adhere to one another. Particles interact because of Brownian (thermal) motion, hydrodynamics, and/or gravitational, Van der Waals, Coulomb, or other forces. During this work, only coagulation due to Brownian motion is considered as this is the dominant mechanism for particle interactions in aerosols. Coagulation due to Brownian motion has been extensively studied and expressions for the rate of coagulation are well known. Furthermore, these expressions have been validated experimentally. [64]

During the development of these expressions it is assumed that upon collision, particles stick together and form a third single spherical particle whose volume is equal to the sum of the original two, i.e., the assumptions are:

- Spherical particles. This assumption implies that the rate of sintering or coalescence is instantaneous compared to the rate of collision. This is a good assumption for very small particles, as shown in Appendix B.
- Accommodation or sticking coefficient of unity. Although little is known quantitatively about the accommodation coefficient of aerosol particles, their low kinetic energies make bounce-off unlikely.

The rate of collision (Z_{ij}) between particles of size υ_i and υ_j is given by $Z_{ij} = \beta_{ij}\, n_i\, n_j$, where n_i is the number of particles of size $\upsilon_{i-1} < \upsilon < \upsilon_i$ per unit volume, and β_{ij} is the collision frequency function. Table 1 gives expression for β_{ij} in the free molecular regime (FMR) and in the continuum regime (CR), when coagulation is due to Brownian motion.

For a monodisperse aerosol with N particles per unit volume, the collision frequency simplifies to $Z = BN^2/2$. Then, the characteristic time for coagulation $\tau_{coll} = N/Z = 2/\beta N$, where τ_{coll} is the average elapsed time between successive collisions for a particle of size υ. It can also be interpreted as the time required to halve the particle concentration of an initially monodisperse aerosol by coagulation, or the time to double the volume of the particles. Table 1 shows expressions for τ_{coll}.

	Collision Frequency Function	Characteristic Time for Coagulation
	β_{ij}	τ_{coll} [s]
FRM	$\left(\frac{6KT}{\rho_p}\right)^{\frac{1}{2}}\left(\frac{1}{r_i^3}+\frac{1}{r_j^3}\right)^{\frac{1}{2}}(r_i+r_j)^2$	$\frac{1}{4N}\sqrt{\frac{\rho}{3KTr}}$
CR	$\left(\frac{2KT}{3\mu}\right)\left(\frac{1}{r_i^3}+\frac{1}{r_j^3}\right)^{\frac{1}{2}}(r_i+r_j)^2$	$\frac{3\mu}{4KTN}$

Table 1. Expressions for the collision frequency function in the free molecular regime (FMR) and continuum regime (CR). [64]

The theory of coagulation is essentially a scheme for keeping account of particle collision as a function of particle size. The rate of formation of particles of size k by collision of particles of size i and j is given by $\frac{1}{2}\Sigma_{i+j=k} Z_{ij}$, where the notation i+j = k indicates that the summation is taken over those collisions for which $\upsilon_k = \upsilon_i+\upsilon_j$. The factor 1/2 is introduced because each collision is counted twice in the summation. The rate of loss of particles of size k by collision with all other particles is $\Sigma_j Z_{kj}$. Hence, the net rate of generation of particles of size k is given by the expression:

$$\frac{dn_k}{dt}=\frac{1}{2}\sum_{i+j=k}\beta_{ij}n_i n_j - n_k\sum_{j=1}^{\infty}\beta_{kj}n_j \tag{1}$$

which is the dynamic equation for the discrete size spectrum when only coagulation is important. The solution of Equation (1) depends on the form of β_{ij}, which is determined by the kinetics of particle collision. In this chapter, the Monte Carlo method developed to solve Equation (1) is described. Initially, a general description of the Monte Carlo technique is presented and then the method is applied to solve the coagulation equation. Later, the model is validated by comparing results with analytical and numerical solutions and experimental observations.

1. Monte Carlo simulation

The Monte Carlo technique is a method of statistically sampling events to determine the average behavior of a system. [65] The name Monte Carlo was first applied to a class of mathematical methods by scientists working on the development of nuclear weapons in Los Alamos in the 1940s. The essence of those methods was the invention of games of chance whose behavior and outcome were used to study statistical and deterministic phenomena. Since then, the term Monte Carlo has been employed to describe a wide range of procedures involving the notion of sampling.

Historically, the first example of a computation by a Monte Carlo method was reported by Buffon in 1777, who described an unexpected method to calculate the value of π. [66] With the increasing availability of very high speed general-purpose computers, many problems have become treatable and the Monte Carlo method has increased in popularity. The technique has

http://dx.doi.org/10.5772/62021

been applied in many disciplines to simulate very diverse systems. The greatest successes of the Monte Carlo method have arisen in areas where the problem itself consists of some random process. It has been applied to simulate problems like chemical kinetics, diffusion, radiation, turbulence, and air pollution.

The solutions obtained through a Monte Carlo simulation are statistical in nature and subject to the laws of chance. This aspect is a drawback, but not a serious one. Convenience, ease, directness, and expressiveness of the method are important assets. Other general features of the method are:

- Cyclic nature of the programming
- Necessity of performing a large series of computations of a uniform type
- Use of a comparatively small amount of memory for storage of intermediate results
- Smoothing of errors

A distinction is sometimes made between *direct simulation* and *Monte Carlo simulation.* In this view, the *direct simulation* is a rather direct transcription into computing terms of a natural stochastic process. *Monte Carlo simulation,* by contrast, is the solution by probabilistic methods of nonprobabilistic problems. The distinction is somewhat useful but often impossible to maintain.

The *direct simulation* replaces the mathematical analysis by a computational algorithm in which the approximations due to the requirements of the mathematical analysis can be avoided. The study of dynamics of gases composed of hard spheres is the classical example. With the direct simulation, the trajectories of molecules are followed by numerically solving the classical equation of motion to predict the location of the particles at successive short intervals of time. At each interval, the system is examined to discover whether collisions have occurred. After every collision, a suitable set of new velocities is given to the particles involved, and the process continues. The changes in velocity distribution, for example are followed by recording the velocity of every particle through many cycles. This application is typical of many in the molecular sciences in that the individual processes (in this case collision) may be quite well understood, but the bulk or average properties cannot be readily related to these events.

With the *Monte Carlo simulation,* the physical problem is replaced by an artificial, probabilistic one. The solution of chemical reaction equations [67] can be used as an illustrative example. In this case, a reactive molecule is represented in the computer by the digit 1. Reaction is indicated by replacing 1's by 0's. To start the reaction, the different storage portions representing each type of molecule are filled with 1's according to their initial concentration. At each step, a random number is generated for each type of molecule being considered. In a second-order reaction, for example, if the numbers 75 and 85 are generated, the 75th molecule type A reacts with the 85th molecule type B by replacing the 1's in each location by 0's. If one or both locations already contain 0's, no reaction occurs. Higher-order reactions, competing reactions, and sequential reactions have been simulated through this technique as well.

1.1. Monte Carlo simulation of aerosol processes

The Monte Carlo method has also been used in the study of aerosol dynamics. Kaplan et al. [68] studied the agglomeration of chain-like combustion aerosols due to Brownian motion. They used the so-called *ising or lattice model,* which has been extensively used in polymer science. This model is a self-avoiding random walk on a lattice, where the state of a particular point in the system depends on the states of its nearest neighbors.

The basic algorithm is as follows: At the beginning of each simulation, monodisperse or lognormally distributed clusters are randomly distributed on the comers of a 2D or 3D lattice. During each time step, each cluster moves at random toward any of the 4 (2D) or 6 (3D) possible directions on the lattice. The probability of movement of a given cluster is dependent upon cluster size as predicted by the diffusion theory; smaller clusters have a proportionately higher probability of diffusion compared to large ones. The probabilities of movement are scaled by assuming the probability of movement of a single mer at, for example, 2000 K to be l. Clusters located on adjacent nodes have a probability of collision that is dependent upon the form of the collision frequency function. At the end of each time step, after each particle has been displaced, and all possible collisions have been checked, the particle size distribution is updated, and the simulation continues until the required time duration is reached. This model accounts only for coagulation, assumes cluster–cluster collisions to be irreversible, and neglects sintering.

Akhtar et al. [69]advanced this work and performed a Monte Carlo simulation of the gas-phase coagulation and sintering of nanosized particles. Particle coagulation and growth were simulated on a 500 x 500 square lattice with periodic boundary conditions to reduce edge effects. During the sintering routine, a particle on any of the perimeter sites of the aggregate is picked at random and allowed to move to any neighboring unoccupied perimeter site on the same aggregate. The probability of acceptance of such movement is determined by the total potential of the new configuration. Configurations with lower total potential are more likely to be accepted. The number of times that a particle is selected (i.e., number of sintering steps) per coagulating step are determined by the ratio of sintering to growth rates.

This method has been successful in providing insight in the formation of agglomerates. However, the possibility of extending it to include coagulation and condensation processes is limited by the weakness of the method in computing the physical time, [69] which is critical in the case of processes occurring at two different timescales like the case of the encapsulation process where coagulation and condensation occurs simultaneously but at different rates.

Instead, coagulation can be simulated through a more straightforward and physical Monte Carlo approach developed by Husar, [55] based on the work of Schaad [67] and Sutherland. [70] In these approaches, position and velocity space are omitted and only collisions are simulated, not in the physical sense but as a transition in a Markov chain. The following section illustrates the concept of Markov chains, and the use of it to simulate coagulation processes.

1.2. The Markov process

A Markov process is a chain of events occurring in sequence with the condition that the probability of each subsequent event in the chain is not influenced by prior events. [71] The usual example is a drunk gentleman who begins a walk through a strange city. At each street comer that he reaches, he continues his walk by choosing completely at random one of the streets leading from the intersection. The history of this random walk is then a Markov chain, because his decision at any point is not influenced by where he has been.

Defining $S_i = \{x_1, x_2,...,x_p\}$ as the set of variables that fully describe the state of a system at time t_i, a Markov chain is defined as the finite set of states $M\{S_1, S_2,...,S_n\}$ through which the system evolves. At each of the discrete sequences of time t_i, the state S_i determines a set of conditional probabilities $q_{i1}, q_{i2},..., q_{im}$, where q_{ij} is the probability that the system which is in state Si, will be in state $S_{i+1} = S_{ij}$ at the (i +l)th time. In other words, q_{ij} is the probability of the transitions $S_i \rightarrow S_{ij}$. It is important to note that the probability of the transition depends only upon the current state S_i and is not affected by the previous history of the system. This is the characteristic *Markovian* property of a process. The state S_f is said to be absorbing if the system remains in this state with probability one. A state S_i is linked with the state S_j if there is a nonzero probability that the system reaches the state S_j in a finite number of steps. A Markov chain is terminating if each of the states S_i is linked to an absorbing state S_f.

In the example of the drunk gentleman in the strange city, the state or position of the gentleman is described by his {x, y} coordinate in the city at every discrete time. The collection of comers where he has been defines the Markov chain. Because of the randomness of his choice at each intersection, the transition probability at each comer is $q_{ij} = q = 1/4$. However, if his choice were determined by his "feeling" of safety, affected for example by the luminosity of the street, or the number of people on the street, the transition probabilities would be different at each state (corner), i.e., $q_{ij} \neq q_{ij+1} \neq q_{mn}$, but his choice would be still unaffected by the places where he has been.

Because of the nature of the problem, it might be possible to simulate a sample walk by playing a roulette wheel with 100 sections. Before every spin, the roulette wheel is divided in 4 sectors, each corresponding to a possible direction, such that each sector has a number of uniformly spaced sections proportional to the sense of safety that the drunk gentleman feels in that specific direction. Starting at a given position, the gentleman's most likely path and most likely position after certain time could be found by simulating a large number of histories, i.e., by running through the process many times. Another example of a Markov process is the coagulation of particles in aerosols.

2. Coagulation as a Markov process

Consider the evolution of an aerosol consisting initially of 5 particles of the same size (singlets). lf the number of singlets in the system at time t_i is denoted by n_{i1}, the number of doublets (particles made of two singlets) by n_{i2}, and so on, the state of the aerosol at the ith time step (collision) is defined by the set Si = $\{n_{i1}, n_{i2},...,n_{is}\}$. Imposing the condition of irreversible collisions, the transition from the. initial state $S_1 = \{5,0,0,0,0\}$ to the final state $S_7 = \{0,0,0,0,1\}$ may proceed along any of the paths shown below.

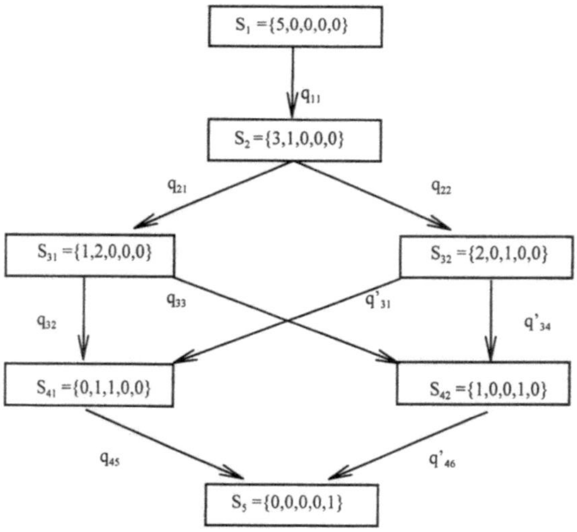

Figure 1. Coagulation as a Markov process. Possible path for the evolution of an aerosol consisting initially of 5 particles of the same size. (From Reference 55).

Every state S_i defines a set of possible types of collisions, each with a probability that is completely uninfluenced by the history of the aerosol. Therefore, the evolution of the aerosol is properly defined as a Markov process.

At time t_1, only collisions among singlets are possible. Then $q_{11} = 0$ for $j \neq 1$. Therefore, the aerosol evolves to the state S_2= {3, 1, 0, 0, 0}. At time t_2, collisions type 1 (among singlets) and type 2 (singles with doublets) will happen with probability q_{21} and q_{22}, respectively. In general, at time t_i a collision type j (particles made of p-singlets with particles made of q-singlets) will occur with probability q_{ij}. The transition probability q_{ij} is proportional to the collision frequency $Z_{pq} = \beta_{pq}\, n_{ip}\, n_{iq}$. With the restriction:

$$\sum_j q_{ij} = 1 \tag{2}$$

then, the transition probability is given by:

$$q_{ij} = \frac{\beta_{pq}\, n_{ip} n_{iq}}{\sum\sum \beta_{pq} n_{ip} n_{iq}} \tag{3}$$

The objective of the Markov-Monte Carlo (Markov-MC) technique is to determine the most likely state at a given time t_i by simulating the transitions S1 S_i, using random or statistical sampling of transitions. At every transition, the sampling of transitions can be done by, for example, aligning the collision probabilities q_{ij} on a 0–1 interval in an arbitrary order and then generating a random number R_n such that $0 < R_n < 1$. Rn identifies uniquely the types of collisions that have occurred, and consequently, the types of transitions that have happened.

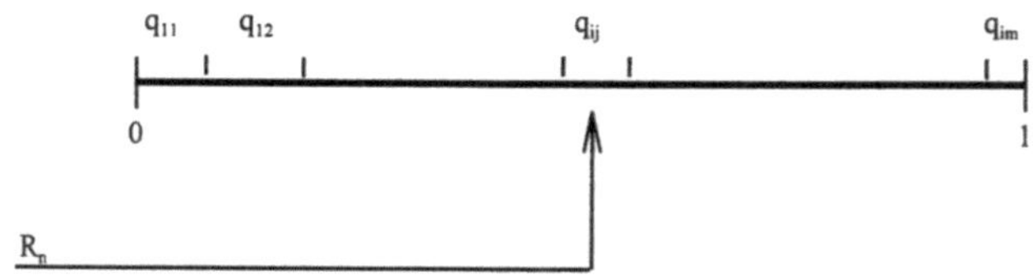

Figure 2. Arbitrary aligning of the transition probabilities in a starting line 0–1 such that a random number will identify uniquely the types of collisions that have happened. (From Reference 55)

Physically, the Markov-MC model simulates particle coagulation by reproducing the following algorithm. Time is divided into time steps. During each time step, the occurrence of every collision is registered and classified according to its type. When the information is normalized by Z, the total number of collisions that have occurred, it provides the probability of occurrence of each type of collision at the given time. This sampling process is Monte Carlo simulated by aligning the probabilities on a O–1 line and generating Z random numbers, each one identifying a type of collision. In other words, by generating Z random numbers and correlating that number to the type of collision being statistically chosen, the collisions that have occurred during the time step are reproduced. Assuming that the time step is short enough, the change in the particle size distribution due to the occurrence of the Z collisions is negligible, and the change can be implemented at the end of the time step with minor error. By decreasing the time step, the error decreases. In the limit, the time step is chosen such that the particle size distribution is updated after every collision.

2.1. Computation of time

Computation of the physical time elapsed between events (i.e., the time step) has been a serious drawback of different Monte Carlo approaches. Most of the past studies have been performed where quantification of time can be avoided. However, when coagulation and condensation occur simultaneously, computation of time is a critical issue.

Schaad [67] proposed to use well-known solutions to calibrate the model with respect to time and then use those settings for the particular case of interest. Using the same approach, Kaplan and Gentry, [68] working with a Monte Carlo simulation to study agglomeration of nonspherical chainlike agglomerates in combustion-generated.aerosols, choose the quantity (N_o/N-1) as a measure by which to represent the rate of cluster growth, since coagulation theory for constant collision frequency functions predicts that this quantity is directly proportional to time. Clearly, these approaches offer reasonable approximations but are not exact.

With the Markov-chain version of the Monte Carlo technique (i.e., the Markov-MC method), the average time between events is computed through the collision frequency function Z_{ij}. Here, an event is defined as a collision among particles of any type. In a unit time and unit volume, there are Z_{11} collisions among partic1es of size 1 and 1 occurring simultaneously with Z_{ij} collisions among particles of size i and j. In total, there are $Z = \Sigma\Sigma\, Z_{ij}$ collisions per unit time and per unit volume.

This implies that in a unit volume, on average there is one collision every 1/Z unit times. Then the average elapsed time between events is given by: [55]

$$\delta t = \frac{1}{\sum_i \sum_j Z_{ij}} \tag{4}$$

If it were desired to simulate the process more rigorously the time increment should be selected from a *Poisson* distribution with the mean corresponding to Equation (4).

The coagulation equation is a time-dependent mass conservation expression for aerosols. Then a numerical solution of this nonlinear integro differential equation can be obtained by updating the particle size distribution function after every Markov-MC simulated collision and by computing the elapsed time through Equation (4). The implementation of this method on a computer code is straightforward. The following section discusses the specific computational aspects involved during its implementation.

3. Description of the code

3.1. Discretization of the particle size range

The Markov-MC algorithm starts by dividing into *m* arbitrary sections the range of particle sizes. A 1D vector (**R**) is used to store this information. The finest grid can be obtained with *dicrete sectionalizations* where section i corresponds to the size of a particle made of i mers. This type of sectionalization is appropriate for the study of the early stages of evolution of, for example, monodisperse aerosols. However, when the evolution of the aerosol is being watched for long periods of time, a sectionalization with a fine grid at smaller sizes together with a coarse gird at larger sizes is more appropriate. This can be done by using a *logarithmic sectionalization* (i α log R_i). Some authors also use a *geometric sectionalization,* where the size of a section i corresponds to a particle with double the mass of the previous section. In other situations, the use of a simple *linear grid* is very convenient. Table 2 shows expressions for the different types of sectionalization.

Type of Sectionalization	Expression
Discrete	$R_i = i^{1/3} R_1$
Logarithmic	$R_i = 10^{1/p} R_1$
Geometric	$R_i = 2^{(i-1)} / R_1^3$
Linear	$R_i = (1 + i / p) R_1$

p parameter to adjust the number of section used according to the range covered

R_i size of the elemental mer, or minimum particle size

Table 2. Expressions for the different types of sectionalization.

http://dx.doi.org/10.5772/62021

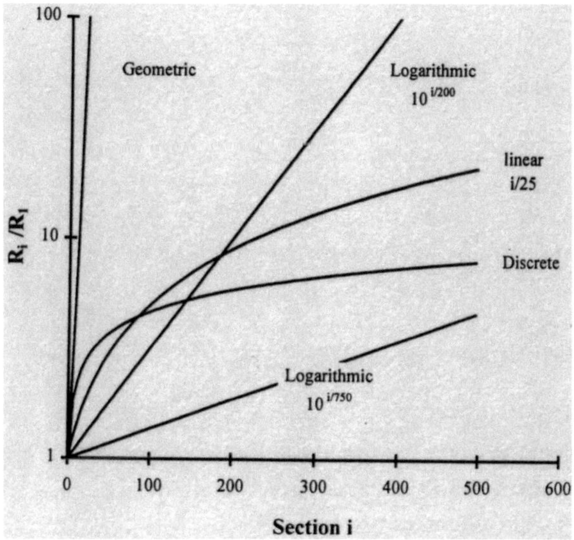

Figure 3. Types of sectionalization used in the Markov-MC model.

3.2. The concept of parcels

In actual combustion aerosols the particle concentration is typically greater than 1 x 10 [18] particles/m3. To directly simulate that many collisions would be impracticable, even with advanced supercomputers. To address this issue the concept of parcel was developed. A parcel is defined as a bundle of $\tilde{n}$ identical particles, i.e., a bundle of particles having the same physicochemical characteristics (size, morphology, and chemical composition). Then, instead of simulating collisions among single particles, collisions among parcels are simulated. Consequently, at every step $\tilde{n}$ collisions of the same type are Markov MC simulated. For a given total number of particles per unit volume {N), the scale factor (f=$N/\tilde{n}$) determines the total number of parcels available during the simulation and thus the statistics of the simulation itself. Greater accuracy is obtained with greater statistics and the statistics of the simulation increases with $\tilde{n}$. Physically, this approach is similar to simulate the process in smaller volumes. By simulating coagulation in, for example, 1 cm^3 instead of 1 m^3, the number of collisions that need to be simulated reduces by 10^6, and the process is still accurately simulated.

3.3. Particle Concentration

Employing the concept of parcels, the discrete version of the particle size distribution (n_i) is stored in a 1D vector (array). n_i is the number of particles per unit volume of size:

$$R_i < r_i \leq R_{i+1} \tag{5}$$

where the actual particle size r_i is given by:

$$r_i = \left(\frac{M_i}{n_i} \frac{3}{4\rho\pi} \right)^{1/3} \tag{6}$$

and M_i is the total mass of the particles in section i. Notice that by using Equation (6), it has been assumed that all the particles within the section have the same size. Also notice that by allowing the size of the particles within a section to dynamically assume their mass mean value, instead of assuming that it remains constant, the total mass of the aerosol is conserved during the simulation of the evolution of the aerosol.

3.4. Aligning of the transition probabilities

In the Markov-MC method, the sampling of transitions between states is done by aligning the collision probabilities q^{ij}'s on a 0-1 interval in an arbitrary order. The implementation of this step is critical because in addition to align the transition probabilities, it should provide an easy and quick way to relate every transition probability q_{ij} with the respective type of collision (i-j).

A 1D vector **P** was used to store the transition probabilities q_{ij}'s and a scheme consisting of a coarse followed by a fine search was adopted to relate q_{ij} to the type of collision that q_{ij} represents. q_{ij} is defined as the probability of occurrence of a collision between particles of size r_i and r_j. We let $r_i \leq r_j$ and define the probability P vector as:

$$\boldsymbol{P}_i = \boldsymbol{P}_{i+1} + \sum_i^m \boldsymbol{q}_{ij} \tag{7}$$

where $\sum q_{ij}$ is the probability that a collision involving a particle of size r_i, with another particle of the same or larger size occurs. P_i is the cumulative probability. A random number R_n between O and 1 will identify the collision that has occurred and a search process involving at most *m* steps (the coarse search) will identify i as the smaller particle involved in the collision. In the fine search, j, the second particle, will be identified through Equation (7) by solving for q_{ij}. This second search requires another *m* operation at most. In contrast, a plain algorithm where every q_{ij} is considered will require up to m2 operations instead of *2m* operations required by the present scheme. A more efficient alternative is desirable since most of the computational time is spent performing this step.

3.5. General algorithm

The overall algorithm to perform the Markov-MC simulation is described in the flow chart shown in Figure 4. Initially, the type of discretization, the starting particle size distribution n_i and the stopping condition (e.g., time for simulation) are specified as inputs to the program. Then, the computation of the collision coefficient β_{ij} for all the possible types of collisions is performed. This information is stored in an *m x m* matrix where *m* is the number of sections

http://dx.doi.org/10.5772/62021

used. Here it is assumed that the collision coefficient is constant within every section, which is a good assumption even with a very coarse sectionalization. This step needs to be performed only once during the entire simulation. Then a loop involving four steps is formed. In the first step, the transition probabilities are calculated and sorted in an array of size *m* representing the probability vector (**P**). In the second, the time step is calculated according to Equation (4). In the third step, a random number (R_n) is generated, the corresponding location on **P** is accessed, and the respective type of collision (i, j) is identified. During the fourth and last step, the particle size distribution function is updated, which involves the withdrawal of one particle from section i and j, and the addition of the new particle to the proper section (k), where $\upsilon_1+\upsilon_j = \upsilon_k$. In the actual code, a utility subroutine to check for mass conservation is used from time to time to search for possible computational errors. These steps are repeated until the stopping condition is reached.

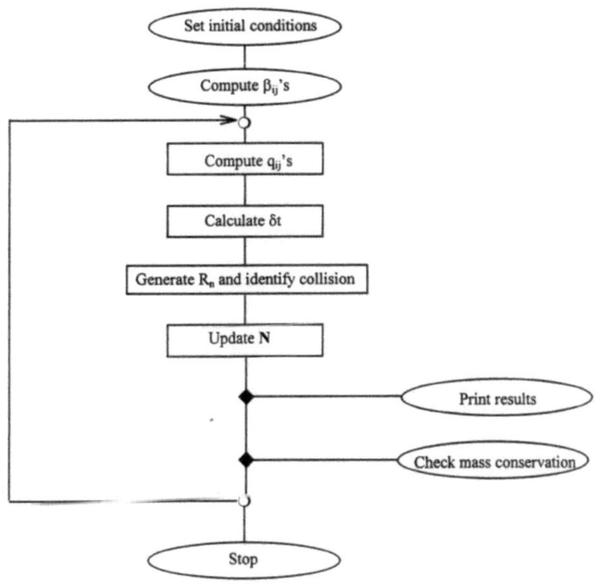

Figure 4. Flow chart illustrating the algorithm for the Monte Carlo simulation of coagulation processes.

4. Validation

Being a probabilistic approach, the calculation of the absolute accuracy of the Markov-MC method is generally impossible. However, its validity can be judged by, for example, comparing results with those obtained by other methods or a model problem whose solution is known accurately. Consequently, in this section the evolution of an initially monodisperse aerosol, with collision frequency function independent of particle size ($\beta_{ij} = \beta$), is Markov-MC simulated and compared to the corresponding analytical solution to test the accuracy of the method. Later, the restriction β = constant will be removed, and the Markov-MC results will be compared with other numerical results and experimental observations.

4.1. Evolution of an initially monodisperse aerosol with β = constant

4.1.1. The Smoluchowski's solution

One of the few analytical solutions to the GDE can be obtained for the case of aerosols subjected to the following restrictions:

- Continuum regime
- Collision frequency function β independent of particle size
- Initially monodisperse size distribution

With these assumptions and setting $r_i = r_j$, the collision frequency function reduces to:

$$\beta_{ij} = k_o = \frac{8KT}{3\mu} \tag{8}$$

Substituting this expression into Equation (1), the coagulation equation reduces to:

$$\frac{dn_k}{dt} = \frac{k_o}{2}\sum_{i+j=k} n_i n_j - k_o n_k \sum_{i=1}^{m} n_i \tag{9}$$

Summing over all values of *k*:

$$\frac{dN}{dt} = -\frac{k_o}{2}N^2 \tag{10}$$

Integrating once,

$$\frac{N}{N_o} = \frac{1}{1 + t/\tau_{coll}} \tag{11}$$

where N_o is the initial total number of particle per unit vo1ume, and τ_{coll} is the characteristic coagulation time given by:

$$\tau_{coll} = \frac{2}{k_o N_o} = \frac{3\mu}{4KTN_o} \tag{12}$$

http://dx.doi.org/10.5772/62021

Physically, the characteristic time for coagulation is the time needed for an initial monodisperse aerosol to reduce the total particle concentration to half of its initial value. To obtain an expression for n_i we proceed inductively, i.e., first an expression for n_1 is obtained, then this result is used to obtain an expression for n_2, and so on. Doing so, the general solution for the concentration of particles of size r_i is:

$$\frac{n_i}{N_o} = \frac{\left(t/\tau_{coll}\right)^{i-1}}{\left(1+t/\tau_{coll}\right)^{i-1}} \tag{13}$$

Evolution of an initially monodisperse aerosol with constant collision frequency function were Markov-MC simulated. Results are shown in Figure 5 along with the analytical solution for N, n_1/N_o, n_2/N_o, and n_3/N_o.The agreement is excellent, demonstrating the validity of the Markov-MC model and the timescaling.

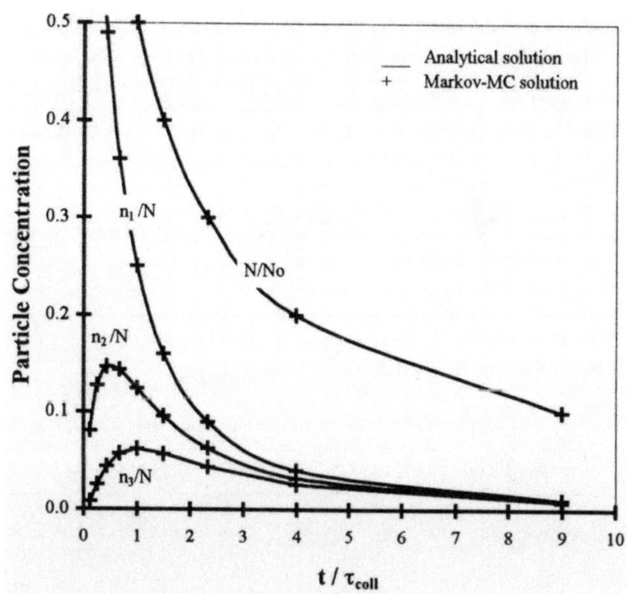

Figure 5. Markov-MC simulation of the evolution of an initially monodisperse aerosol with collision frequency function β independent of particle size. Good agreement between Markov-MC simulation results and the analytical solution are obtained.

Figure 6 shows the error in the total number of particles per unit volume at different stages of the evolution. The error in all cases is below 1% for $t/\tau_{coll}<10$, showing a good agreement between the analytical solution and the Markov-MC simulation. The error arises from the computation of the time steps through Equation (4). This error can be minimized up to any degree by increasing the statistics of the simulation, i.e., by increasing the number of parcels $\tilde{n}$ available during the simulation. However, simulations with higher $\tilde{n}$'s use greater amount of computational resources. Figure 6 illustrates the effect of $\tilde{n}$ on the error. It shows that the error is cumulative and increases exponentially with evolution.

The increase in error with time results because with every event (collision), the number of parcels available for simulation decreases by one. Consequently, the statistics of the simulation decreases with the number of events performed and, thus, the error in the computation of the time steps increases. The cumulative error in time can be maintained below a certain level without increasing the use of computational resources by dividing the entire simulation into several sequential runs. A run is stopped before the cumulative error in time is excessive. Before the next subsequent run, the number of parcels in each section is multiplied by 1O and the scale factor *f* is divided by 10, so that the total number of particles is conserved and the statistics of the simulation is increased. This practice allows the evolution of the aerosol to be carried out over very long periods of time, while minimizing the error in the computation of time and minimizing the use of computational resources.

To determine the appropriate initial number of parcel $\tilde{n}$ to use during every run, several Markov MC simulations were conducted varying $\tilde{n}$. A balance between high statistics and use of computational resources was sought. Table 3 and Figure 6 show the results obtained. The values on Table 3 were obtained running the code on *Charney*, a NASA-Cray J932 machine, able to operate at 4.0 gigaflops. Flops is the number of floating point operations performed per second and a floating point operation is defined as any operation that manipulates numbers expressed in floating point notation. [72]

f	Number of Starting Parcel ñ	System CPU [s]	User CPU [s]
1x10 [12]	$1x10^6$	1.4954	447.1
1x10 [13]	$1x10^5$	0.3904	260.9
1x10 [14]	$1x10^4$	0.2713	6.8
1x10 [15]	$1x10^3$	0.2224	3.2

Table 3. Simulation of the evolution of an initially monodisperse aerosol with N_o=1x10 [18] particles/m^3.

In Table 3, the Central Processing Unit (CPU) time is the amount of system time required to run the job, i.e., the number of seconds devoted to system operations required for the program. The user CPU time is the amount of time that the program requires of the CPU.

Figure 6 and Table 3 show that working with Charney, the balance between accuracy and use of computational resources is obtained by starting with 1 x 10^6 parcels and increasing the resolution every 0.9 x 10^6 events. However, the required number of starting parcels depends on the machine used and the number of sections actively being used. For example, early stages of the evolution of the monodisperse aerosol require less computational operations than a fully developed one, since at the early stages most of the sections are empty, and the number of operations per event is proportional to the number of sections being actively used. On the other

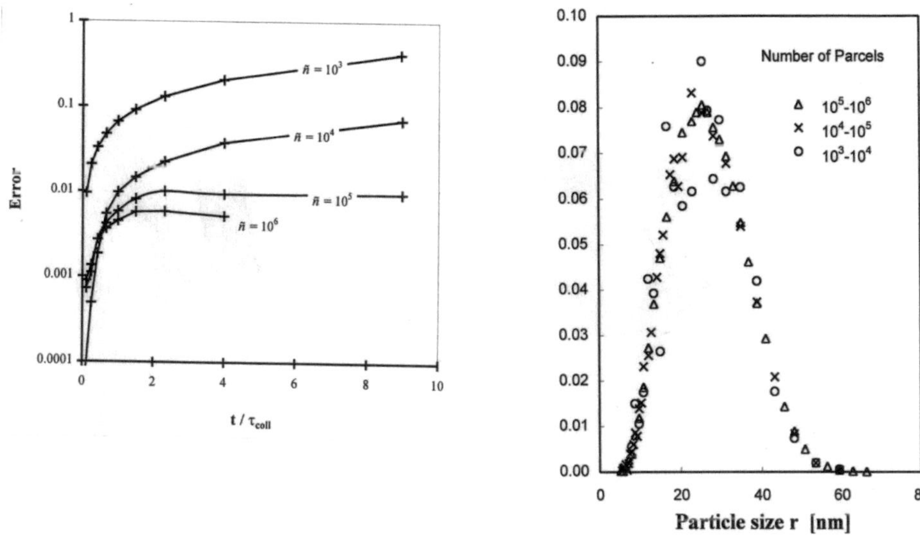

(a) (b)

Figure 6. (a) Error of the Markov-MC method in computing the total number of particles per unit volume at different stages of the evolution of an initially monodisperse aerosol with constant collision frequency function β. (b) Comparative error in the evolution of an initially normal distributed aerosol as function of the initial number of parcels ñ used.

hand, working with slower machines, resolution needs to be sacrificed to obtain results within a reasonable amount of time. For example, to obtain results within an hour, the number of starting parcels need to be reduced to 1×10^5 for *Megalon,* a local UNIX machine, while for a PC 110 MHz, the number of starting parcels need to be reduced to 1×10^4.

4.1.2. *Effect of the types of sectionalization and random number sequence*

Several runs were made to observe the effect of different types of sectionalization on the Markov MC results. For the same conditions, discrete, geometric, linear, and logarithmic sectionalization was used. In all the cases, the results were the same. The possibility of using different types of sectionalization according to the problem being analyzed constitutes another advantage of the Markov-MC method over similar codes like the sectional method, which was designed to work on a logarithm type of sectionalization. A similar type of test was performed to see the effect of the number of sections being used on the evolution of a coagulating aerosol.

The evolution of an initially normal distributed aerosol was observed using a logarithmic type of sectionalization. Several runs were made, varying the number of section per decade being used. Figure 7.a shows the results obtained. This figure shows that the number of sections per decade can be reduced up to 18 and the evolution of the aerosol as predicted by the Markov-MC model is basically the same.

Similarly, the effect of the random number sequence being used was studied. C++, as any other programming language, provides a standard library function to generate pseudo random numbers with a uniform distribution. The sequence of random numbers produced by this function is determined by a seed number. Varying this seed number, different sequences can be obtained. Figure 7.b shows the Markov-MC results obtained for the evolution of an aerosol for three different random number sequences. Figure 7.b shows that the Markov-MC results are independent of the sequence of random numbers used.

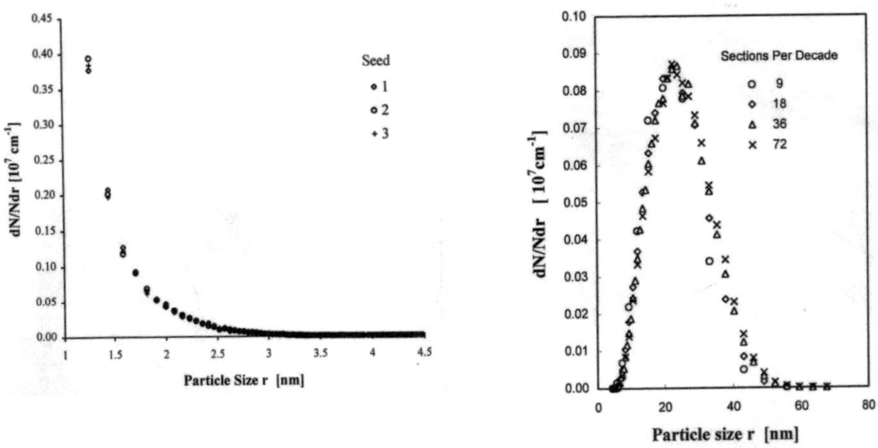

(a) (b)

Figure 7. (a) Size distribution at an arbitrary time for an initially normal distributed aerosol as predicted by the Markov-MC model using a logarithmic type of sectionalization with different numbers of sections per decade. (b) Size distribution at $t/\tau_{coll} = 45.3$ ($\tau_{coll} = 49\mu s$) for an initially monodisperse aerosol ($N_o = 4.6 \times 10$ [19] particles/m^3, $r_1 = 1nm$) as predicted by Markov-MC method using three different random number sequences (seeds).

4.2. Comparison with numerical and experimental results

In general, the collision frequency function β is not a constant but depends on the sizes of the colliding particles and the nature of the aerosol. Under these conditions, there is not an exact analytical solution to the coagulation equation. Many numerical and experimental works have been performed to describe the behavior of coagulating aerosols. The main results are summarized here.

Later, the Markov-MC results obtained for an atmospheric aerosol with β(r) are qualitatively compared with these numerical and experimental results.

Friedlander et al. [52] stated that the particle size distribution in a coagulating aerosol approaches an asymptotic self-preserving form after long periods of time, and appears to be independent of the initial size distribution. The self-preserving distribution for the case of β = constant is exponential in form, whereas the self-preserving distribution for Brownian coagulation appears to be lognormal. Thus, for Brownian coagulating aerosols, the state of the aerosol at any time could be characterized by only two parameters, the mean particle size and the geometric standard deviation $\sigma_{g.}$

The theory was later supported by Hidy [73] who through numerical experiments concluded that the self-preserving form develops after about 3 dimensionless coagulation times ($3\tau_{coll}$) and that the shape of the asymptotic distribution varies with the Knudsen number (K_n) but not with the initial conditions. Later, Lee et al. [74] assumed a lognormal type of self-preserving distribution and found an approximate analytical solution for the coagulation equation by using the method of moments. The solution predicts an asymptotic value of $\sigma_g = 1.38$ in the free molecular regime. The solution also estimates the time to reach the asymptotic distribution in the range from 0 to $473\tau_{coll}$ depending on the initial conditions.

Matsoukas and Friedlander, [75] studying the dynamics of the formation of metal oxides (MgO and ZnO) in a flat flame where salts of magnesium and zinc were introduced in the form of a dry aerosol, measured the particle size distribution of samples collected at different heights above the flame. They observed that the distribution collapses into a single curve when plotted in normalized form and concluded that the normalized distribution is, to a good approximation, lognormal with a geometric standard deviation $\sigma_g \cong 1.4$. Similarly, Megaridis, [76] studying the morphology of the soot formed in a coannular ethane diffusion flame, obtained a value for $\sigma_g = 1.39–1.46$. Akhtar et al., [77] studying formation of TiO_2 by gas-phase synthesis, observed that the mean particle size evolves logarithmically while the geometric standard deviation moves very quickly toward $\sigma_g \cong 1.4$.

To validate the Markov-MC method, results for a coagulating atmospheric aerosol (i.e., water in air at room temperature) with β(r) were obtained and compared with these numerical and experimental results. Initially, the aerosol consists of $N_o = 1 \times 10$ [18] water particles/m^3 of 1 nm in radii.

Figure 8 shows the evolution of the aerosol as predicted by the Markov-MC method. The results are presented in terms of nondimensional particle size distribution (n_i/N) as a function of the nondimensional time (t/τ_{coll}). The characteristic time for collision at the initial conditions is used to nondimensionalize time. Figure 8 shows that the particle size distribution gradually broadens out with time and evolves toward a self-preserving distribution that seems to be lognormal.

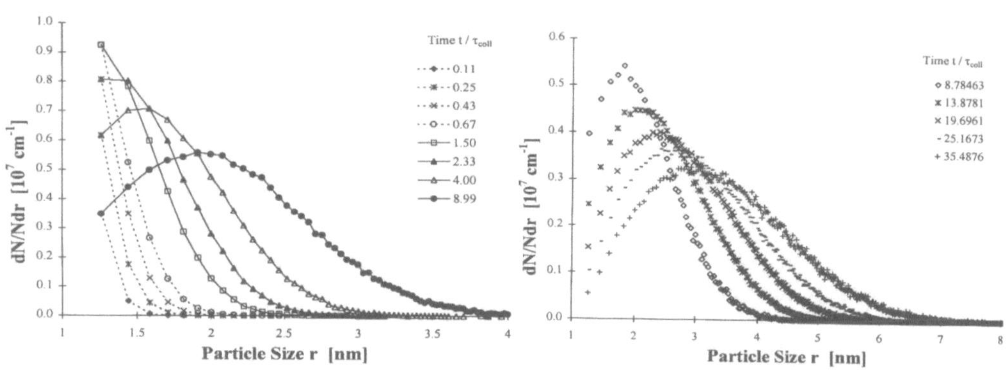

Figure 8. Size distribution of an initially monodisperse aerosol ($N_o = 1 \times 10$ [18] particles/m^3, $r_1 = 1$ nm, $\tau_{coll} = 2.25$ ms) as predicted by the Markov-MC method. The aerosol approaches a lognormal distribution after $\cong \tau_{coll.}$

To determine the type of self-preserving distribution predicted by the Markov-MC method, the obtained Markov-MC distributions were fitted with different exponential distribution functions. The goodness-of-fit was evaluated by the *chi-square test*, [64, 78] and it was found that among the exponential distributions, the lognormal distribution function produced the best fit to the data. The mean particle size r_m and the geometric standard deviation σ_g of the lognormal distribution were evaluated and Figure 9 shows the values of r_m and σ_g obtained as a function of time. This figure shows that the mean size r evolves logarithmically and the geometric standard deviation σ_g moves very quickly toward $\sigma_g \cong 1.45$, in agreement with other numerical and experimental observations.

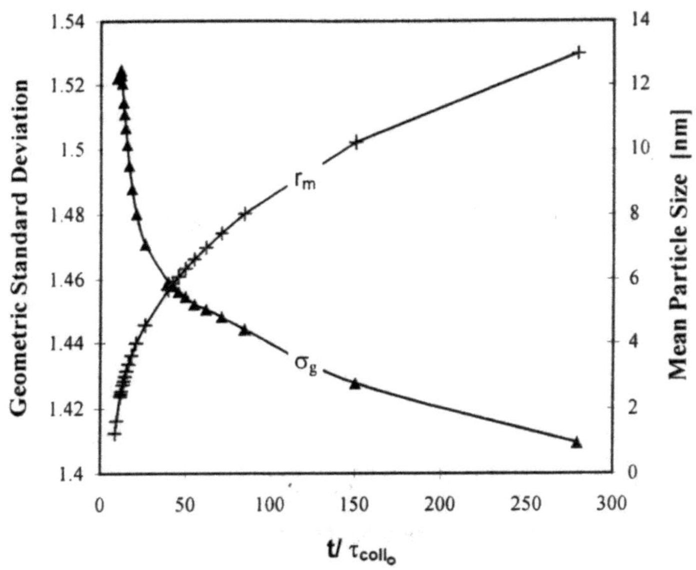

Figure 9. Evolution of the mean particle size r_m and the geometric standard deviation σ_g of the particle size distribution as predicted by the Markov-MC method, assuming that the distributions are lognormal.

5. Overview

A Monte Carlo method has been developed to simulate particle collisions in aerosols. Collisions are simulated as transitions in a Markov chain. The Markov-Monte Carlo (Markov-MC) method has been validated by comparing results with analytical and numerical results and with experimental observations. The method can handle any number of sections and any type of sectionalization. Conditions to obtain good accuracy with minimum use of computational resources were determined. The convenience, ease, directness, and expressiveness are some of the advantages of the method. However, the unique advantages of the Markov-MC method appear when condensation processes are added into the model. This is the subject of the next chapter.

http://dx.doi.org/10.5772/62021

Author details

Jose Ignacio Huertas

Address all correspondence to: jhuertas@itesm.mx

Tecnológico de Monterrey, Mexico

Section 5

Condensation

Chapter 5

Incorporating Condensation into the Markov-MC Model

Jose Ignacio Huertas

Additional information is available at the end of the chapter

http://dx.doi.org/10.5772/62020

In this chapter, the differential equations governing the growth of particles by condensation in the continuum regime (CR) and free molecular regime (FMR) are presented. Then, the methodology used to couple the solutions of the condensation equations with the Markov-MC simulation of the coagulation equation is described. This approach exploits the advantage of the Markov-MC method in allowing a cross-linking of deterministic and probabilistic models. In the present case, coagulation, which is modeled from a probabilistic approach, is combined with condensation, which is modeled deterministically. Since the two processes occur simultaneously, they are coupled through time. The coupling is carried out by using the time step for coagulation as the delta time for condensation. Thus, during every coagulating time step, the extent of growth by condensation of each particle in the aerosol is evaluated, and the particle size distribution is updated according to the new sizes of the particles. The results presented here initially focus on situations where only condensation is important, and later on, situations in which both processes, coagulation and condensation, occur simultaneously.

1. Condensation

When a droplet is embedded in a sufficiently supersaturated environment, the droplet grows by condensation of vapor on its surface. Diffusion theory and the kinetic theory are respectively used to calculate the rate of condensation in the CR and FMR. The expressions are known as the *growth laws* [50] and are presented in Table 1. The rate of growth is controlled by the rate of arrival of vapor molecules at the droplet surface. It is proportional to the vapor concentration difference that exists between the surface of the particle and far away from the particle. The exponential term in the growth laws describes the vapor phase concentration at the surface of the particle.

$$P = P_s \, Exp\left(\frac{2\sigma M}{\rho RTr}\right) \tag{1}$$

Equation (1) is well known as the Kelvin equation. It is a relationship that expresses the vapor pressure over a curved interface in terms of the saturation pressure P_s, which is the vapor pressure of the same substance over a flat surface. The vapor pressure of a liquid is determined by the energy necessary to detach a molecule from the surface by overcoming the attractive force exerted by its neighbors. When a curved interface exists, as in a small droplet, there are fewer molecules immediately adjacent to a molecule on the surface than when the surface is flat. Consequently, it requires less energy for molecules on the surface of a small drop to escape and the vapor pressure over a curved interface is greater than that over a plane surface. [64] The Kelvin effect is significant for particles smaller than 0.1 μm in diameter.

There is a critical particle size r* where the concentration gradient becomes zero and thus the growth laws predict no net rate of condensation. Under this condition, the system is in a metastable condition, where the rate of evaporation equals the rate of condensation. The growth laws show that all smaller particles ($r < r^*$) evaporate while all the larger ones ($r > r^*$) grow by condensation. The growth laws are obtained assuming that the condensation rate is sufficiently slow for the latent heat of condensation to be dissipated without changing the droplet temperature. Appendix A develops a heat transfer model to evaluate the accuracy of this assumption, and Chapter 6 presents the implications on the condensation rate when the increase in the droplet temperature is not negligible. Here the discussion is limited to situations where the assumption is reasonable. The growth laws can be expressed in terms of nondimensional variables η, S, and τ as shown in Table 1 by using $\eta = r/r^*$, $S = P/P_s$, and $\tau = t/\tau_{cond}$, where r* is critical particle size for the onset of condensation; P is the vapor pressure of the condensable phase; Ps its saturation pressure; and τ_{cond} the characteristic time for condensation. Physically, $3\tau_{cond}$ is the time required to double the volume of a particle of size r* by condensation. Expressions for τ_{cond} are also presented in Table 1.

	Free Molecular Regime	**Continuum Regime**
Rate of growth	$\frac{d_r}{dt}=\frac{1}{\rho\sqrt{2\pi RT/M}}\left(P-P_s{*}Exp\left(\frac{2\sigma v_m}{rKT}\right)\right)$	$\frac{d_r}{dt}=\frac{1}{r}\frac{DM}{RT}\left(P-P_s{*}Exp\left(\frac{2\sigma v_m}{rKT}\right)\right)$
Nondimensional form	$\frac{d_\eta}{d\tau}=\frac{1}{Ln(S)}\left(1-S^{\frac{1}{\eta}-1}\right)$	$\frac{d_\eta}{d\tau}=\frac{1}{Ln(S)}\frac{1}{\eta}\left(1-S^{\frac{1}{\eta}-1}\right)$
Characteristic time for condensation	$\tau_{cond}=\frac{\rho r^*\sqrt{2\pi RT/M}}{P_sSLn(S)}$	$\tau_{cond}=\frac{\rho RT r^{*2}}{DM P_sSLn(S)}$
Solution for $\eta\to 1$	$\eta=1+(\eta_o-1)S^{\frac{t}{\tau_{cond}}}$	$(\eta-\eta_o)+Ln\left(\left\lvert\frac{\eta-1}{\eta_o-1}\right\rvert\right)==\frac{t}{\tau_{cond}}$
Solution for $\eta\to\infty$	$\eta-\eta_o=\frac{S-1}{S\ Ln(S)}\frac{t}{\tau_{cond}}$	$\eta^2-\eta_o^2=2{*}\frac{S-1}{S\ Ln(S)}\frac{t}{\tau_{cond}}$

Table 1. Expressions for the rate of particle growth.

Assuming constant vapor concentration and temperature, the nondimensional versions of the growth laws were numerically integrated for several values of S. The results are presented in

Figure 1. Figure 1a shows the evolution of particle size in the FMR and Figure lb for the CR. Three characteristic regions can be distinguished in each figure. For small sizes, $\eta \to 1$, the Kelvin effect is important and particle growth is slow. For large sizes, $\eta \to \infty$, the Kelvin effect is negligible and particles grow linearly with time in the FMR (Figure 1a) or as the square root of time in the CR (Figure 1b). In between these two extremes, there is a transition region.

Analytical solutions can be obtained in each of the two extreme cases. Table l presents these solutions. For the case of $\to \infty$, the rate of growth equation becomes linear and then it can be directly integrated. For the case of $\eta \to 1$, , the solution is obtained by expanding the exponential term of the growth equation in a Taylor series around η = 1, as follows:

$$1 - S^{\frac{1}{\eta}-1} = Ln(S)^{*}(\eta - 1) + \text{HOT} \tag{2}$$

Then, after neglecting higher-order terms (HOT), the equation is reduced to a linear ODE that can be integrated analytically. The expressions obtained are shown in Table l. The generalized condensation solutions were obtained assuming that the droplet is embedded in an infinite medium such that the concentration of the condensable material remains constant during the entire process. The assumption is relaxed by dividing the total elapsed time for condensation into several time steps (δt_{cond}) such that $\delta t_{cond} \ll \tau_{cond}$ and by updating the vapor phase concentration at every time step, i.e., by reducing the mass in vapor phase of the condensable material by the amount of mass condensed during each time step.

2. Coupling the condensation solution to the Markov-MC simulation of coagulation

The following discussion applies to two-component aerosols composed of a fully condensed material (solid or liquid) and a condensable material. Thus, condensation of only one of the components needs to be considered. Situations where the two components are condensable phases, or where there are more than two components, can be handled by a direct extension of this method but they will not be considered in this work.

It is assumed that a particle in the two-component aerosol can be described by its size (r) and mass fraction (y) of the condensable material present in the particle. Size and composition of a particle are given by:

$$r = \left(\frac{3}{4\pi} \sum \frac{m_k}{\rho_k} \right)^{1/3} \tag{3}$$

$$y = \frac{m_2}{\sum m_k} \tag{4}$$

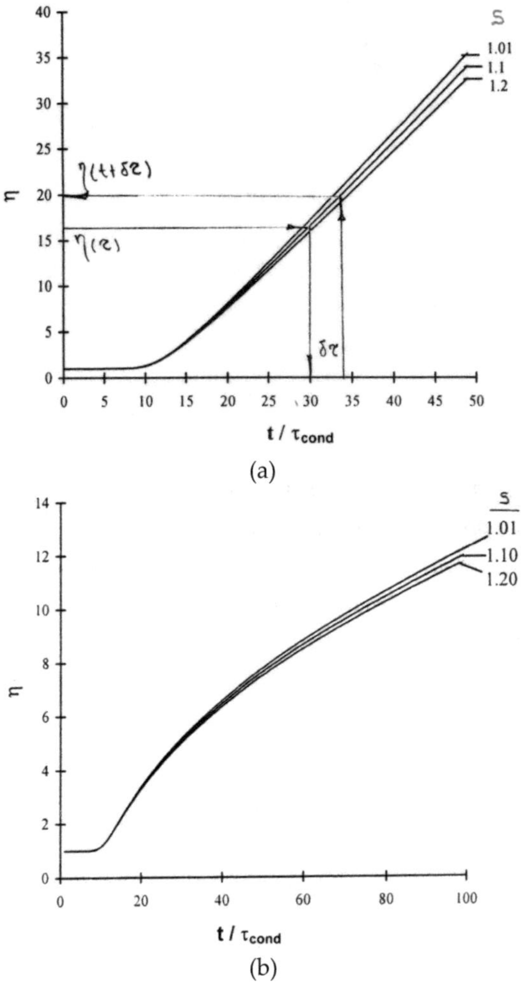

Figure 1. Numerical solution of the particle growth laws in the (a) FMR and (b) CR. Use of the universal solutions to evaluate particle growth due condensation for an arbitrary initial particle size, during a given nondimensional time $\delta\tau$ and saturation ratio S.

where m_k and ϱ_k are the mass and density of species k in the particle. We will let k = 1 represent the fully condensed material and k = 2 represent the condensable material.

The particle size range (R_1-R_m) is divided into *m* sections, and the particle composition range ($Y_1 = 0$ - $Y_p = 1$) into *p* sections. A particle within a section (i, j) has a size r such that $R < r < R_i$ $_{+1}$ and composition y such as $Y_j < y < Y_{j+1}$ It is assumed that all particles within a section (, j) have the same size and composition, and equal to the temporal values of the mass weighted mean size (r) and mean composition (y) of the particles within the section. Thus, these mean values can vary within their respective ranges in the section. The mean values r and y are computed from Equations (3) and (4), respectively, by using m_k. as the mean mass of species k in the particle and according to:

http://dx.doi.org/10.5772/62020

$$m_k = \frac{M_{ijk}}{n_{ij}} \tag{5}$$

where M_{ijk} is the total mass of specie k in section (i, j), and n_{ij} is the number of particles in section (i,j). This methodology has three important characteristics:

1. The particles within a size-section have different sizes and different compositions. Only particles within a size-composition-section have same size and composition.

2. Mass is conserved since size and composition within a section are allowed to assume their instantaneous mean values.

3. There is no restriction about the structure of the particles. In Chapter 6, as a special case, it will be assumed that the particles consist of a solid core with a spherical coating.

Since coagulation and condensation processes occur at the same time, the Markov-MC simulation of the coagulation equation and the deterministic solution of the condensation equation must be coupled through time. This suggests the use of the following type of algorithm:

1. Perform a Markov-MC coagulating step as described in Chapter 4

2. Compute the time step for coagulation δt_{coll} from Equation (4 from Chapter 4) and use this time step as the elapsed time for condensation δt_{cond}

3. For each particle in the aerosol

   - Compute the growth during δt_{cond}

   - Update the particle size distribution by moving the particle to the appropriate section according to its size and composition

4. Update vapor concentration to account for the condensed mass

Thus, this technique requires the evaluation of the particle growth equation for all particles in the aerosol with size greater than r* for each coagulating time step. Consequently, a direct numerical integration of the growth laws for the specific conditions of each particle would be computationally prohibitive. Instead, the nondimensional version of the particle growth laws can be solved for a range of values of S, as described in the former section. These solutions can then be stored in tables or can be represented by curve-fits for the different solutions. Thus, during the actual run, the direct numerical evaluation of the integral expression is replaced by a table-lookup process or an evaluation of the curve-fitting expression. Evaluation of particle growth for an arbitrary initial particle size η_o, nondimensional time step $\delta\tau$, and vapor concentration S using the generalized solution, through either table searching or evaluation of curve-fitted expressions, can be obtained by:

$$\delta\eta = \int_{\tau_0}^{\tau_0+\delta\tau} \frac{d\eta}{dt}dt = \int_{0}^{\tau_0+\delta\tau} \frac{d\eta}{dt}dt - \int_{0}^{\tau_0} \frac{d\eta}{dt}dt \tag{6}$$

$$\delta\eta = \eta_{0-\tau_0+\delta\tau} - \eta_{0-\tau_0} \tag{7}$$

where $\eta_{o-\tau}$ is the tabulated universal value for growth due to condensation during τ nondimensional times. The process is illustrated in Figure 1.

3. Results

A two-component aerosol will behave quite differently when the characteristic time for coagulation is greater than or less than the characteristic time for condensation. Thus, we define J as:

$$J = \frac{\tau_{coll}}{\tau_{cond}} \tag{8}$$

Expressions for J in the CR and FMR are presented in Table 2. J is a function of temperature and is proportional to $S^*Ln^{\alpha}(S)/N$ in both regimes.

Free Molecular Regime	Continuum Regime
$J = \frac{1}{16\sigma}\sqrt{\frac{KT}{3\pi\sigma}}\frac{P_s SL\ n^{\frac{5}{2}}(S)}{N}$	$J = \frac{3\mu D}{16\sigma^2 v_m}\frac{P_s SL\ n^3(S)}{N}$

Table 2. Expression for J, the ratio of the characteristic time for coagulation and the characteristic time for condensation.

The condition $J \to \infty$ designates situations where only condensation is important and $J \to 0$ designates situation where only coagulation occurs. The following sections describe the results obtained for $J \to \infty$, $J \to 0$ and $J \sim 1$.

3.1. Results for $J \to \infty$

The performance of the Markov-MC method for simulating an aerosol subject to condensation but not coagulation was evaluated. A lognormal distributed aerosol with parameters $r_m = 3.0$ nm, N = 10 [18] particles/m^3, and $\sigma_g = 1.45$ was taken as the initial particle size distribution.

Condensation was assumed to occur in the FMR and a vapor with S = 1.2 and $r_o^* = 3.9$ nm was considered.

Figure 2 shows the results obtained with a) S = constant and no Kelvin effect, b) vapor phase mass depletion and no Kelvin effect, and c) vapor phase mass depletion and Kelvin effect. Since r* is the critical size above which condensation occurs, there is a discontinuity in the particle size distribution at $r = r_o^*$. When the Kelvin effect is neglected and the concentration of the vapor remains constant, the tail of the particle distribution above r* is observed to steadily increase, appearing as equally spaced parallel curves (Figure 2a). This result is expected because particle growth is independent of size in the FMR when the Kelvin effect is negligible. Figure 2a also shows that the Markov-MC method is able to handle discontinuities in size distribution and does not suffer from numerical dispersion or diffusion as is the case with the sectional method. [60]

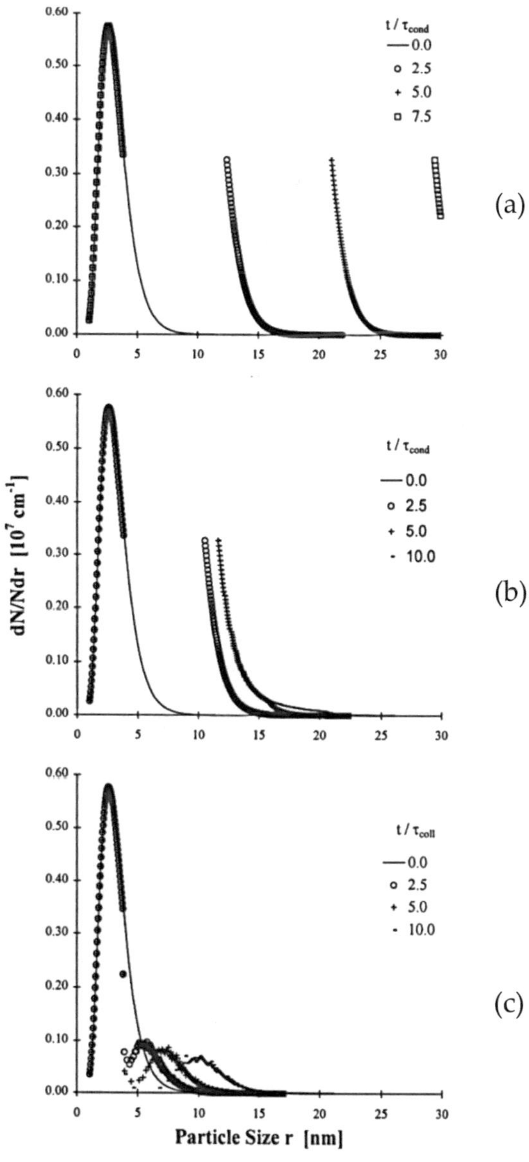

Figure 2. Evolution of an aerosol in the FMR when only condensation is important for the case of (a) S = constant and no Kelvin effect, (b) vapor phase mass depletion and no Kelvin effect, and (c) vapor phase mass depletion and Kelvin effect. The initial conditions is a lognormal distributed aerosol with parameters r_m = 3.0 nm, N = 10 [18] particles/m^3, and σ_g = 1.45 and a vapor with S = 1.2 and r_o* = 3.9 nm. The solid line is the initial particle size distribution.

Figure 2b shows the corresponding evolution when the mass of the condensable vapor is depleted as condensation occurs. Two additional effects are observed. First, as condensation takes place, the rate of growth slows down and then, the distributions are no longer equispaced in time. Second, as condensation proceeds, S decreases, r* becomes larger (Figure 3), and then the growth of the particles with sizes $r_o^* < r < r^*$ diminishes and the particle size is frozen.

For the same conditions but including the Kelvin effect, Figure 2c shows the slow growth of particles with sizes close to r*. The evolution of the aerosol can be described as the superposition of the lognormal distribution tail over the exponential variation with size of the Kelvin effect, which leads to bimodal distributions. Due to the Kelvin effect, small particles ($r \cong r^*$) grow slowly and larger particles grow faster, in an exponential relation with size. Therefore, the concentration of particles widens more strongly at the smaller sizes, and thus the particle size distribution (particle concentration per unit size) diminishes more strongly at smaller sizes. Furthermore, when the particles reach size $r > \sim 5r^*$, the Kelvin effect becomes negligible and particles grow at the same rate. Thus, the spreading effect stops first for the larger particles. The net effect is the formation of the bimodal distribution.

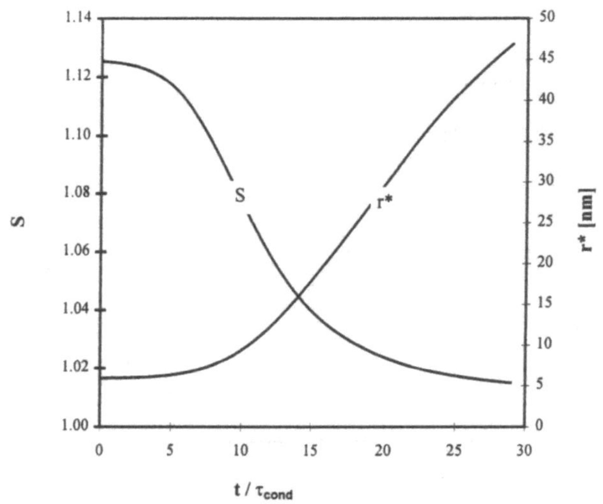

Figure 3. Evolution of S and r* during condensation for the conditions for an initially lognormal distributed aerosol with parameters r_m = 3.0 nm, N = 10 [18] particles/m³, and σ_g = 1.45 and a vapor with S = 1.2 and r_o^* = 5.9 nm.

3.1.1. Evolution of a single particle

To have a better understanding of the effect of gas-phase depletion on particle size evolution, tagged particles have been observed during the condensation process. Figure 4 shows their behavior. For a particle with initial size close to r_o^*, say $\eta = r/r_o^* = 1.01$, the growth is strongly affected by the Kelvin effect and the particle grows very slowly. As the particle becomes larger, the Kelvin effect is less important, and the particle grows faster. As the condensable material is depleted, particle growth slows down and the particle starts to approach its asymptotic size which is reached when the condition S = 1 reached. However, before that equilibrium condition is reached r* can be larger than the particle size, and consequently its growth is frozen. In this model reevaporation processes has not been considered and thus the particle maintains its maximum size. The larger particles, e.g., η_o = 1.18 and η_o = 1.35, exhibit similar behavior initially. However, the cumulative influence of the Kelvin effect separates particle sizes.

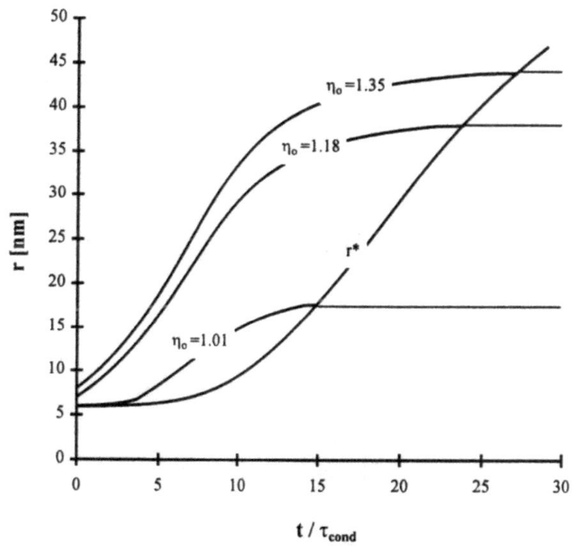

Figure 4. Evolution of tag particles during condensation. Initially, the particle is subject to the Kelvin effect. At the end, gas-phase depletion slows down particle growth and the particle approaches asymptotically its final equilibrium size.

When condensation occurs in the FMR over all the particles in the aerosol, i.e., when $r_m >> r^*$, the particle size distribution is not affected by condensation provided that S = const. However, when vapor-phase mass depletion is considered, the condensation process widens the particle size distribution during the final stages of the process. On the other hand, condensation in the CR is proportional to (1/r) and then condensation causes the particle size distribution to narrow.

The literature review of Section 3.3.2 concluded that most of the problems of the numerical methods for modeling aerosols arise when coagulation and condensation occur simultaneously. The next section describes the results obtained when the Markov-MC method is used to simulate simultaneous coagulation and condensation in a single-component aerosol. Results for twocomponent aerosols will be presented in Chapter 6.

3.2. Results for J = 0.18

The results presented are for an atmospheric aerosol in the FMR. Initially, the particles have a lognormal distribution with r_m = 1.85 nm and σ_g = 1.56. The vapor concentration is assumed to remain constant with parameters S = 1.2 and r* = 5.9 nm. The results were obtained using a linear grid with 1000 sections to cover the range 1–20 nm. The evolution of the aerosol is described in terms of the parameters r, $\tau = t/\tau_{cond}$, n/N, and *J*.

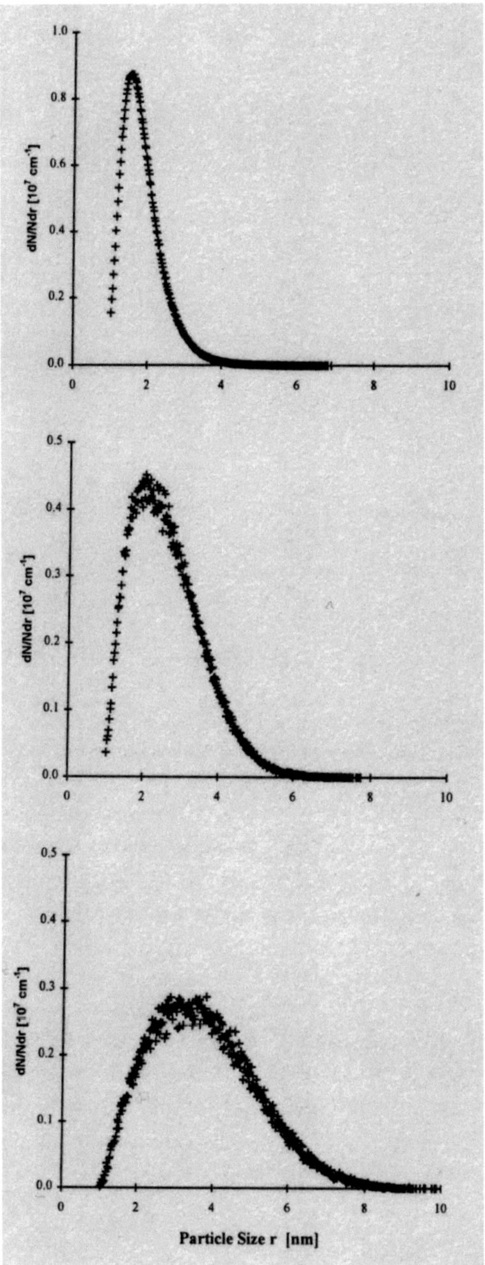

Figure 5. State of evolution of an atmospheric aerosol (a) τ = 43, (b) τ = 765, and (c) τ = 2500. The initial condition is a lognormal distributed aerosol with parameters r_m = 1.85 nm, N_o = 10 [21] particles/m^3 and σ_g = 1.56; vapor with constant concentration and parameters S = 1.2 and r* = 5.9 nm. J = 0.18 (τ_{cond} = 7.87 x 10^{-6} s).

http://dx.doi.org/10.5772/62020

For $J = 0.18$, Figure 5 shows the state of evolution of the aerosol at $\tau = 42$, 765, and 2500. The initial particle concentration is $N_0 = 10$ [21] particles/m^3 and the characteristic time for condensation is $\tau_{cond} = 7.87 \times 10^{-6}$ s. Under these circumstances the rate of condensation, even though high, is small compared to the rate of coagulation ($\tau_{coll} = 9.27 \times 10^{-7}$ s). Therefore, the effect of condensation on the particle size distribution is negligible, as shown in Figure 5.The evolution of the aerosol is similar to that discussed in Section 4.4.2 when only coagulation is important.

3.3. Results for J = 1.18

Keeping the same set of conditions, but decreasing N_0 up to 10 [20] particles/m^3 so that $J = 1.18$, the effect of condensation on the particle size distribution begins to be important, as shown in Figure 6. In this case, the aerosol exhibits a pseudo bimodal distribution, which can be explained as follows: The Kelvin effect dictates that particles with $r > r^*$ grow by condensation but smaller particles will not. Then condensation results in a bulk motion of the distribution toward larger sizes for $r > r^*$, creating a gap in the distribution around r^*. Particle concentration does not change due to condensation but coagulation depletes the concentration of small particles and increases the concentration of the larger ones. Part of the coagulating particles partially fills the gap created by condensation. The combined effect is shown in Figure 6.

During the evolution of the aerosol, the model keeps track of the composition of the particles. For each particle, it distinguishes the mass coming from condensation from the mass coming from coagulation. For single-component aerosols, as in this case, particle composition is defined as the ratio of the mass of the particle due to condensation over the total mass of the particle. Figure 7 shows the average size-composition distribution of the aerosol at $\tau = 3320$. It shows that particles with $r < r^*$ are formed through pure coagulating processes. Particles with sizes slightly larger than the critical size are affected by the Kelvin effect and thus the content of the condensed phase is small but increases with particle size. A maximum is reached and then for larger particles, the mass ratio decreases due to further coagulation with smaller particles, i.e., with particles that have not received mass through condensation.

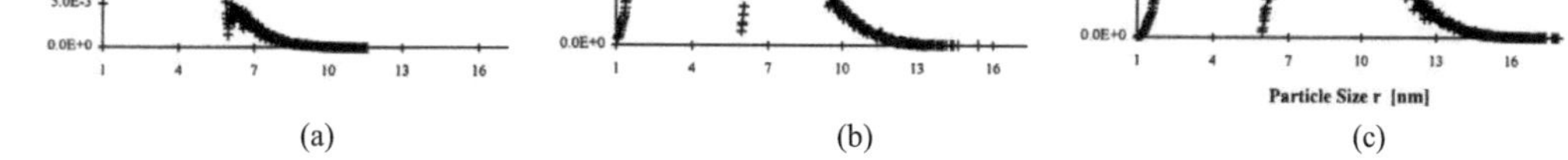

Figure 6. State of evolution of an atmospheric aerosol (a) $\tau = 630$, (b) $\tau = 2075$, and (c) $\tau = 3320$. The initial condition is a lognormal distributed aerosol with parameters $r_m = 1.85$ nm, $N_o = 10$ [20] particles/m^3, and $\sigma_g = 1.56$; vapor with constant concentration and parameter $S = 1.2$ and $r^* = 5.9$ nm. $J = 1.18$ ($\tau_{cond} = 7.87 \times 10^{-6}$ s).

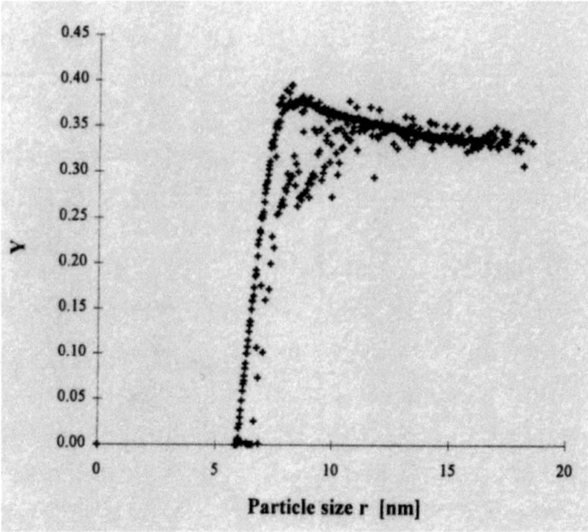

Figure 7. Particle size-composition distribution at τ = 3320 for an initially lognormal distributed atmospheric aerosol subject to condensation.

4. Concluding remarks

It has been shown that the Markov-MC method is an effective approach to modeling aerosol dynamics under conditions of pure coagulation, pure condensation, and when both coagulation and condensation occur simultaneously. Because the Markov-MC method does not have restrictions in the number of sections used, the particle size distribution of aerosols can be represented with high resolution. It also can be applied to broad particle size ranges and can evaluate the evolution of aerosols over long time periods.

The method is accurate in solving the condensation equation in multicomponent aerosols because it evaluates the growth of each particle in the aerosol at the time, and in doing such evaluation it uses generic exact solutions of the condensation equation. The errors introduced come from the methodology used to store the exact solutions of the particle growth equation. However, this process can be optimized up to any degree of accuracy as desired. Furthermore, when the Kelvin effect can be neglected, analytical expressions are available and no errors are introduced during this step. This approach can be extended to include other aerosol processes such as source/removal, and chemical reactions. The assumptions made for coagulation and condensation are summarized as follows:

1. Particles are spherical and stick together upon collision

2. Rate of condensation and coagulation independent of particle composition

3. Particles within an (i, j) section have the same, but not constant, size, and composition

In the following chapter, the Markov-MC method will be applied to a two-component aerosol to study the particle encapsulation process.

http://dx.doi.org/10.5772/62020

Author details

Jose Ignacio Huertas

Address all correspondence to: jhuertas@itesm.mx

Tecnológico de Monterrey, Mexico

Section 6

The Particle Encapsulation Process

Chapter 6

The Particle Encapsulation Process

Jose Ignacio Huertas

Additional information is available at the end of the chapter

http://dx.doi.org/10.5772/62019

The aim of this chapter is to model and study the encapsulation process described in Chapter 1 as an alternative to control contamination and agglomeration of flame-synthesized nanosized particles. The aerosol formed during the production of nanosized powders in sodium/halide flames is composed of M, NaCl, and Ar, where M is a metal or ceramic. This type of aerosol is characterized by very high particle concentrations (~10^{18} particles/m^3) and high temperatures (>1000°C). Furthermore, the M/NaCl/Ar aerosol is a two-component aerosol, since both M and NaCl are condensable phases.

Particle formation in flame is affected by many factors that make a complete analysis of this process extremely complicated. Particle dynamics, chemical kinetics, heat and mass transfer fields are some of the factors that affect the final product. Despite these complications, considerable insight can be gained by focusing attention on aerosol dynamics alone and considering the burner as an idealized plug flow reactor in which the relevant gas-phase chemistry and transport are decoupled from the particle dynamics. The characteristics of the final particles, for example, size distribution and morphology, are primarily affected by coagulation and condensation, i.e., by aerosol dynamics.

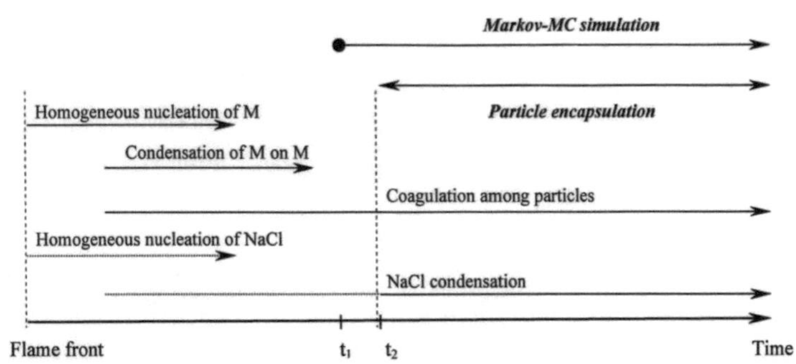

Figure 1. Chronology of events occurring during particle formation in M/NaCl/Ar aerosols. Dashed lines indicate the processes that need to be suppressed to favor encapsulation of M particles.

Particle formation in M/NaCl/Ar aerosols involves the formation and growth of M and NaCl particles by nucleation, condensation, and coagulation. Figure 1 illustrates the processes involved and their sequence. Since NaCl is the more volatile material, encapsulation of M particles will occur, either directly when the NaCl vapor condenses onto the M particles producing NaCl-coated M particles, or indirectly when uncoated particles coagulate with the coated particles.

To describe the evolution of the aerosol when condensing NaCl vapor encapsulates the M particles, the Markov-MC model developed in Chapters 4 and 5 is applied to the M/NaCl/Ar aerosol. This work leads to identifying the controlling mechanisms and variables that affect the particle size distribution (PSD) and the M particles size distribution (MPSD). Furthermore, the model allows the optimum conditions for particle encapsulation to be identified.

1. General description of the aerosol process in a sodium/halide flame

Consider the case where reactant gases MCl_m and Na diluted in inert are mixed and react producing a flame. The products of combustion are the primary (core) material M (e.g., Ti), inert (e.g., Ar), and a condensable material, NaCl, which will serve as the encapsulating material. The overall chemistry for this class of exothermic reactions is:

$$MCl_m + mNa \rightarrow mNaCl + M \qquad (1)$$

In the flame sheet limit, the flame can be considered as an infinitesimally thin surface where reactions take place at an infinite rate. The products of combustion form the M/NaCl/Ar combustion aerosol. The temperature of the particles within the aerosol is approximately equal to the temperature of the surrounding gases. The flame temperatures considered can be well below the melting point of the metal or ceramic M. For example, for TiC_4, Na and 90% Ar introduced at 700°C and a pressure of 1 atm, the adiabatic flame temperature is 1053°C. The products of combustion under these conditions are Ti in solid phase (T_m = 1668°C for Ti) and NaCl in vapor phase.

When the temperature of the aerosol is well below the saturation temperature of the M material, it nucleates and condenses. However, under these circumstances, classical homogeneous nucleation theory may not model accurately the nucleation and condensation of the M material, since this theory uses macroscopic physical properties to describe entities made of few atoms. However, since the encapsulation process is not directly affected by nucleation of M, here it is simply assumed that nucleation and condensation of M has been completed well before the onset of NaCl condensation. An. initial size distribution for M will be assumed and the importance of this assumed distribution to the conclusions will be evaluated. Figure 1 illustrates the processes that will be included in the encapsulation study. In the vicinity of the flame front, the NaCl vapor is unsaturated, and therefore coagulation of the M particles is the dominant process. Downstream of the flame front the temperature drops due to heat transfer and heat loss. When the aerosol temperature drops below the NaCl saturation temperature, the vapor condenses onto the M particles producing NaCl-coated M particles. However, not all the existing particles are coated as explained below.

According to the classical theory of homogeneous condensation, supersaturated vapors will condense if appropriate nuclei are present. The vapor can either create its own nuclei (homogeneous nucleation) or use the existing particles in the aerosol as nuclei of condensation (heterogeneous condensation). The Kelvin effect, discussed in Chapter 5, requires that only nuclei with size greater than a critical size r* can serve as condensation nuclei (r* is defined by Equation 1 from Chapter 5). When S is higher than a critical value (S_{crit}), the concentration of clusters of size r* that are self-generated by the vapor becomes significant and catastrophic homogeneous nucleation occurs (expressions for S_{crit} can be found in Reference 79). On the other hand, when S is less than S_{crit} the number of clusters of size $r > r^*$ is negligible. Therefore, for a given temperature, a metastable condition is maintained and condensation will not occur. For the case considered, when the M particles grow to size $r > r^*$, heterogeneous condensation will occur over these "core" particles producing NaCl-coated M particles.

Temperature and vapor concentration of the condensable material must thus be controlled to avoid homogeneous nucleation of NaCl and favor encapsulation of particles through heterogeneous condensation. Rates of heterogeneous condensation must also be fast enough to ensure heavy coatings before subsequent collisions. This type of coating will separate the cores from each other during subsequent collisions, inhibiting the agglomeration of M particles. The range of temperatures and partial pressures of NaCl for which the encapsulation process can occur as described above can be understood by referring to Figure 2. To the right of the saturation pressure curve, NaCl is in a stable unsaturated condition ($S<1$) and will not condense out regardless of the core particle size. To the left of the homogeneous nucleation curve, NaCl is in a supersaturated condition such that $S>S_{crit}$ and NaCl can form its own nuclei and homogeneously condense out. Between these two curves ($1<S<S_{crit}$) heterogeneous condensation can take place.

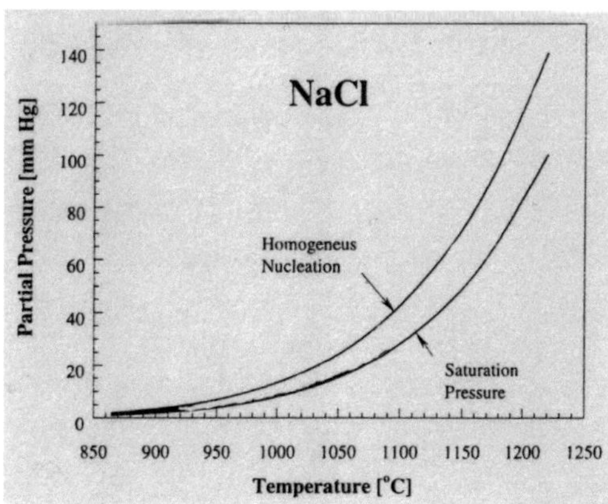

Figure 2. Homogeneous nucleation and saturation pressure curves for NaCl. To the right of the saturation pressure curve, NaCl is unsaturated ($S<1$) and cannot condense out. To the left of the homogeneous nucleation curve, NaCl is supersaturated ($S>S_{crit}$) and will homogeneously condense out. Between these two curves ($1<S<S_{crit}$) heterogeneous condensation can take place.

While the above discussion is useful in conceptualizing the encapsulation process, particle dynamics has not been considered. In the next section, a more accurate description is obtained by simulating condensation and condensation with the Markov-MC model.

2. Modeling particle encapsulation

The particle encapsulation process in its simplest form is a two-component process that involves two phenomena: particle coagulation and vapor-phase condensation. The governing equations, physical description, and methods of solution for these two processes were presented in Chapters 4 and 5. The modeling of the particle encapsulation process reduces to solving the governing equation through the Markov-MC model under appropriate assumptions and conditions. The description of these assumptions and conditions follows.

2.1. Particle morphology

When two coated particles collide they stick together with a probability α, which is known as the accommodation coefficient. At the contact point of the two spheres, a neck is formed whose size increases with time. For the initial stage, the rate of growth is driven by the curvature gradients in the neck region. For intermediate sintering or coalescing rates, the curvature gradient diminishes and the surface free energy becomes the driving force for continued sintering. At this stage, the motion is induced by the tendency of the interface to reduce its area in order to minimize the interfacial energy. Appendix B presents a description about the mechanisms of particle sintering in microscopic materials. Nonetheless, this information provides an insight in the mechanisms of sintering of nanosized particles.

When the rate of sintering ($1/\tau_{sint}$) of a newly formed particle is much higher than the rate of particle collision, i.e., $\tau_{sint} << \tau_{coll}$, it can be assumed that at any time during the aerosol evolution, the particles are spherical. For uncoated M particles, the spheroidicity of the particles is limited by the rate of sintering of these particles. For coated particles, it is limited by the rate of sintering of the condensed phase, e.g., NaCl. Table 1 shows the characteristic time for sintering of Ti and W in crystal phase and NaCl in liquid phase for several values of particle size. The characteristic times for sintering were obtained assuming that the Ti and W sinter by solid-state diffusion, while NaCl particles coalesce by the viscous flow mechanism. Table 1 shows that the rates of sintering for NaCl droplets and Ti crystal particles are several orders of magnitude faster than collision rates. Then, for the size range considered, it can be concluded that the spheroidicity of the particles is a reasonable assumption. Table 1 also shows that for Ti at 1100°C, particles with size r < 50 nm poses a characteristic sintering time several orders of magnitude shorter than typical experimental resident times (~1s). Thus, no agglomerated structures should be formed while the particle size is 20–40 nm in radii. This conclusion agrees with the SEM and TEM micrographs presented in Chapter 2.

According to the previous discussion, it will be assumed than the particles in the M/NaCl/Ar aerosol are spherical and consist of M cores particles embedded within a NaCl droplet. A

http://dx.doi.org/10.5772/62019

Size r [nm]	τ_{coll} [μs]	τ_{sint} [μs]	
		Ti (c)	NaCl (l)
3.8	214	0.01	3.73×10^{-3}
5.9	674	0.04	5.78×10^{-3}
15.0	730	0.71	1.45×10^{-2}
50.0	1380	27.2	4.90×10^{-2}
100.0	5530	216.0	9.76×10^{-2}

Table 1. Characteristic time for sintering of Ti particles in crystal phase and NaCl in liquid phase at 1100°C, compared to the characteristic time for collision of Ti particles at 1100°C. $N_{Ti} = 10^{18}$ particles/m³ when r = 3.8 nm.

particle is described by its equivalent size r and its composition Y, where r is the radius of the particle as a whole and Y is the ratio of NaCl mass and the total mass in the particle. The condition Y = 0 describes a pure M particle, while Y = 1 a pure NaCl particle. When either a coated and uncoated particle or two coated particles collide, two types of structures are possible as shown in Figure 3.

In the first type, NaCl mass fraction of the colliding particles is low ($Y \to 0$) and the two cores are in contact upon collision. Assuming that the sintering of the two cores is nearly instantaneous, a new spherical particle is formed with size and composition determined by the size and composition of the colliding particles.

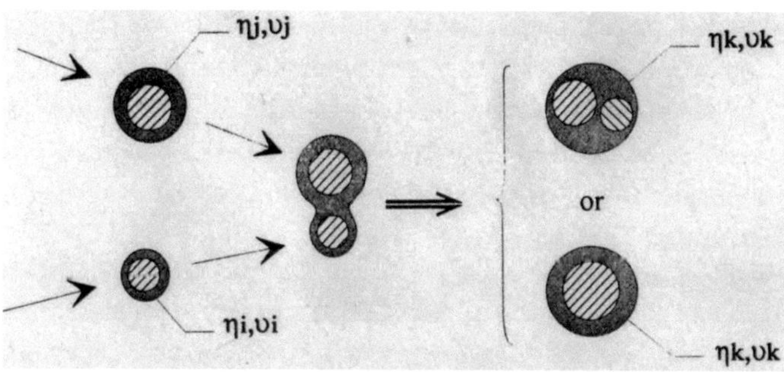

Figure 3. Possible structures formed after collision of particles.

In the second type, the NaCl mass fraction of the colliding particles is high ($Y \to 1$). The heavy coating on one or both of the particles isolates the cores from each other. The liquid-phase coating of the newly formed particle coalesces instantaneously and a spherical particle with two cores is formed.

However, the cores within the liquid NaCl droplet are subject to Brownian motion and can potentially collide and sinter. Whether the cores within the liquid phase collide or not depends on several factors: NaCl mass fraction (Y), core sizes (r_c), residence time (τ_{res}), and temperature (T) are the dominant ones. T affects the rate of Brownian motion, while Y affects the length scale for collision, yielding a timescale for collision of cores in the liquid phase τ_B. The condition ($Y \to 1$) combined with ($\tau_{res} \to 0$) favors final double core particles.

A criterion to determine the amount of coating material required to avoid embedded-core collisions can be obtained from relating the characteristic two-core collision time τ_B to the particle residence time $\tau_{res.}$ The residence time is defined as the time spent by the particle at temperatures higher than that of the melting point of the condensable material. For typical experimental conditions the order of magnitude of τ_{res} is ~ 1s. The condition $\tau_B << \tau_{res}$ leads to the potential that the core particles will contact one another within the NaCl matrix, while $\tau_B >> \tau_{res}$ leads to two separate core particles.

To evaluate the likelihood that the cores will collide, the theory of particle coagulation is applied to a colloidal system made of two equal-sized cores encapsulated in a liquid droplet. The average time for the two cores to collide τ_B is defined in Appendix C as $\tau_B = \mu\pi r^3/8KT$, where r is the total size of the final particle (core plus coating). This model neglects the enhancing effect of the boundaries of the liquid droplet in the rate of collision of the two cores. The model shows that τ_B is independent of the initial core size, and has a linear variation with the volume available for motion of the cores. Table 2 shows the values obtained at different conditions of temperature, and particle size. From Table 2 it can be concluded that the cores within the NaCl liquid droplet collide in a timescale similar to the timescale for collision of the particles in the aerosol, i.e., $\tau_B \sim \tau_{coll.}$ Though the particle diffusion velocities are much lower in the liquid phase, the distances between particles are also much lower.

This approximate analysis also predicts that two Ti cores within NaCl droplets of size r < 100 nm will come in contact within a timescale much shorter than the typical experimental residence time. Whether or not these core particles will sinter or coalesce depends on the conditions within the droplet. Experimental results suggest that low melting point metals (e.g., Ti) coalesce, while hotter melting point materials (e.g., AlN) do not show evidence of sintering and appear to remain as separate core particles. The behavior of core particles upon low velocity collision in a salt matrix will require more attention but is beyond the scope of this work.

(NaCl+M) Droplet of Size r [nm]	τ_B [μs]	
	1100°C	800°C
10	9.38×10^{-1}	1.27×10^{0}
25	1.47×10^{1}	1.98×10^{1}
50	1.17×10^{2}	1.58×10^{2}
100	9.38×10^{2}	1.27×10^{3}
250	1.47×10^{4}	1.98×10^{4}

Table 2. Characteristic time for collision of two equal-sized core particles encapsulated within an (NaCl+M) droplet of size r.

Much insight can be gained by considering extreme conditions, i.e., assuming that 1) the cores always collide and coalesce (equilibrium solution) and 2) the cores never collide or coalesce (frozen solution). The equilibrium solution refers to the results obtained when it is assumed that upon collision of coated particles, a new coated particle with a single core is formed, while the frozen solution refers to the results obtained when it is assumed that the NaCl particle coating prevents collisions or sintering of the cores of the colliding particles. The equilibrium solution overestimates the size of the cores because it enhances coagulation of M cores while the frozen solution underestimates the size because it limits coagulation of the M cores.

2.2. Particle heating during condensation

The theory of condensation described in Chapter 5 assumes constant temperature aerosols. However, particles warm up as the latent heat of vaporization is released during the process of condensation. Usually it is argued that the increase in temperature is negligible, but most of these arguments are for modest condensation rates and for particles in the CR. This issue becomes even more important when it is realized that the rate of condensation is a strong function of S, and S at the particle surface is a strong function of particle temperature. For example, a 3.2°C change in temperature of NaCl vapor at 1100°C decreases S from 1.01 to 0.98. Thus, small temperature variations could result in a very different condensation behavior. Figure 4 illustrates the variation in S when a constant mass of vapor changes temperature.

To characterize the magnitude of the particle temperature increase during condensation, a heat transfer model was developed for both regimes, FMR and CR (see Appendix A). Here, only the conclusions for the FMR are described. As a first step, the analysis assumes that the conditions of the vapor far from the particle remain constant. An energy balance is performed and the resulting equation is solved coupled to the rate of condensation equation.

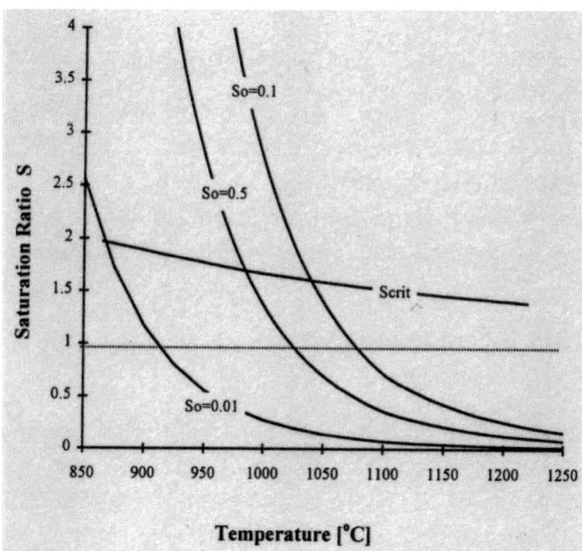

Figure 4. Variation of the saturation ratio (S) with temperature for the same mass of NaCl. S_0 is the saturation ratio at 1250°C.

Figure 5 shows the increase in temperature of a Ti particle with size r* as it grows by condensation of NaCl vapor at 1100°C when the rate of condensation is affected by particle heating. The condensation process rapidly approaches a steady-state condition, where the rate of convective heat loss balances the rate of latent heat released. The steady-state condition is established because the thermal resistance of the coated particle is much less than the convective thermal resistance and because the fraction of the energy released needed to heat the coated particle is negligible. Thus, the particle heats instantaneously and the system does not have thermal inertia.

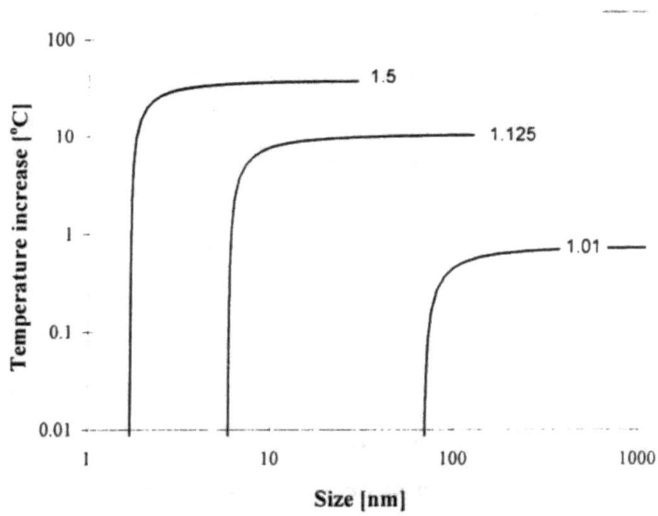

Figure 5. Increase in temperature for Ti particle during condensation of NaCl vapor at 1100°C and S = 1.5, 1.125, and 1.010.

Figure 5 can be understood as follows: energy dissipation by convection is proportional to the increase in particle temperature δT, where $\delta T = T_p - T_\infty$, and the rate of heat release is proportional to the rate of condensation. Thus, δT is proportional to the rate of condensation. The rate of condensation is affected by the Kelvin effect when r~r*, and is thus a function of particle size.

Consequently, for a given S and T, the increase in particle temperature δT is a function of size and there is a unique δT for given size.

The rate of condensation in the FMR is independent of particle size when the Kelvin effect is negligible, and thus a steady-state condition is reached when the particles are sufficiently large. At this state, the particles assume a constant maximum temperature δT_{max} independent of particle size and despite further condensation. The results of Figure 5 and Table 3 show that particles in the FMR undergo a significant increase in temperature for high values of S_∞, i.e., for high rates of condensation. They also shows that neglecting particle heating the growth by condensation is overestimated by a factor of ~4.

S_∞	δT_{max}	m	$m_{w/o}/m$
1.01	0.81	0.25	3.88
1.125	9.86	0.23	4.00
1.5	37.5	0.18	4.44

m = rate of condensation in the FMR when the Kelvin effect is negligible

w/o = without correction for particle heating

Table 3. Particle temperature increase in FMR with particle heating for NaCl at 1100°C.

Thus far, only the local effects of the latent heat release during high rates of condensation have been considered. This energy heats the particles and, consequently, limits the rate of condensation. Another limiting effect on the rate of condensation is found when the global effect of the latent heat release is considered. In adiabatic systems or in systems where the rate of heat loss (q_{loss}) is smaller than the rate of latent heat release, the entire aerosol heats up during the condensation process, as described by the following energy balance:

$$H_v \sum_i n_i \rho_i \frac{dv_i}{dt} = q_{loss} + \sum_i m_i C_{pi} \frac{dT}{dt} \tag{2}$$

where H_v is the latent heat release per unit mass, ρ_i is the density of i in condensed phase, dv_i / dt is the rate of condensation for size I, m_i is total mass of i per unit volume of aerosol where i represents each species in the aerosol including inert, vapor, and condensed phases, and T the global temperature of the aerosol.

As shown in Figure 4, when the global temperature increases, the saturation ratio (S) decreases. The rate of condensation would decrease with time in an adiabatic system, and thus, heat loss plays a critical role in defining the rate of condensation. These two effects were incorporated in the Markov-MC model.

2.3. Wetting effects

When heterogeneous condensation occurs, the condensable phase condenses out on particles made of a different material. The vapor and molecular clusters of the condensable material are absorbed onto the surface of the "foreign" particles, wetting the surface. Once the foreign particles possess a thin coating, the vapor phase does not recognize the identity of the foreign particles and the particles behave as nuclei made of the condensable material. Then condensation proceeds as predicted by the growth law equations described in Chapter 5.

The assumption of this description is that a wetted foreign particle can be obtained. However, hydrophobic solid surfaces are not wetted in such a way that a continuous stable liquid film is formed. The extent of wetting is given by the difference between adhesive (solid–liquid interface) and cohesive (liquid–liquid) forces, and thus a very diverse wetting phenomenon can be observed depending on the materials involved. The study of particle wetting is out of the scope of this work. Herein it is assumed that the onset of heterogeneous condensation is unaffected by wetting effects, i.e., the condensation growth laws are applicable to the uncoated particles. This assumption implies that NaCl wets the primary particles and that the cohesive forces are negligible compared to the adhesive forces. Figure 2-9 shows a NaCl-encapsulated Ti particle indicating that NaCl effectively wets Ti particles.

2.4. Working regime

For typical experimental conditions of M/NaCl/Ar aerosols, $0.01 < Kn < 10.0$. Therefore, the well-known Fuchs-Sutugin correction factor for condensation and coagulation in the transition regime was included. Implementation of more accurate correlations is straightforward.

2.5. Initial conditions

The controlling variables of the particle encapsulation process in sodium/halide flames are inlet temperature and reactant concentrations. Flame temperature, M mass, and NaCl concentration are determined by stoichiometry, energy conservation, mass conservation, and physical properties of the constituents. Therefore, T and S at the flame front can be taken as the controlling variables for simplicity in the study of the aerosol dynamics.

When NaCl is the encapsulating material, the range of temperatures of interest for atmospheric pressure flames is between 800°C and 1400°C. Flame temperatures can be controlled by reactant dilution and/or by controlling the temperature and phase of the reactants at the inlet of the reactor. Values for the saturation ratio of the condensable vapor range from 1 to S_{crit}. For NaCl, $S = 2$ is the upper boundary for S_{crit} over a wide range of temperatures as shown in Figure 4.

On the other hand, when the initial S and T are defined, the total mass of the M material is given by stoichiometry. The concentration of M particles (N) is obtained by assuming a particle size distribution (e.g., monodisperse, normal or lognormal) and mass conservation. The initial distribution for the M particles is simply assumed since it is not necessary to accurately predict nucleation to model encapsulation. For each of the cases studied, several runs were made to observe the effect of the initial particle size distribution on the evolution of the aerosol. For the same mass, normal and lognormal distributions were used as the initial condition. For most of the cases the results were qualitatively similar. Therefore, for every case studied, only a typical behavior is presented and discussed.

3. Results

This section presents the results obtained when the Markov-MC model is applied to a Ti/NaCl/Ar aerosol under the assumptions and range of initial conditions described above. This study is intended to allow for an understanding of the dominant mechanism involved in the nanoencapsulation process and to demonstrate the usefulness of the model in studying two-component aerosols. Two cases will be considered: constant temperature and constant heat loss. The constant temperature case will be considered to introduce the salient features of nanoencapsulation; nonetheless, heat loss which is intrinsic to most flame systems, will be shown to be of fundamental importance in controlling nano-encapsulation.

The results are not expected to yield quantitative agreement with the experiments as the flame has a complex two-dimensional structure and we will assume a uniform aerosol that evolves with time. Nonetheless, we expect the model to elucidate the essential features of nano-encapsulation. We will study the nano-encapsulation process for one case that is similar to the typical conditions of the sodium/halide flame for which there are experimental results as shown in Chapter 2.

3.1. Encapsulation at constant temperature

The constant temperature condition applies to very dilute aerosols or to systems where the rate of latent heat release can be dissipated as it is generated. As an initial study, we will consider the case where a sudden encapsulation occurs in the preexisting aerosol. The aerosol will be subjected to a step change in saturation ratio as might be experienced in flames, expansion shock waves, mixing, or sudden drops in temperature. The main characteristics of the encapsulation process under these conditions will be delineated by considering the evolution of a Ti/NaCl/Ar combustion aerosol. Initially, the aerosol is assumed to consist of a lognormal distribution of pure Ti particles in a supersaturated gas-phase mixture of NaCl with S = 1.125 and T = 1100°C. The parameters of the lognormal distribution are $r_m = 1.86$ nm, $\sigma_g = 1.45$. For these conditions, the total particle concentration is $N = 1.6 \times 10^{19}$ particles/m^3.

Figure 6 shows the evolution of the aerosol. Under the chosen initial conditions $r^* > r_m$ and only the upper tail of the distribution is initially affected by condensation. Since the Kelvin effect mandates that condensation growth rates are lower for smaller particles, condensation elongates the upper tail of the distribution and creates a gap around r*. At the same time, the concentration of the vapor decreases, r* increases, and the rate of condensation slows down. Coagulation fills in the gap and increases the concentration of particles in the upper tail, creating a bimodal distribution. Since the global temperature of the aerosol remains constant and there is no source of condensing material, condensation soon ceases to be important, and coagulation becomes the dominant process. Eventually, coagulation smoothes the distribution, and it approaches a lognormal type.

Figure 7 shows the variation with time of S and r*. It is seen from the figure that condensation is only important for a short initial period of time. S changes from 1.125 to ~1.02 within one millisecond. After that, a condition of slight supersaturation remains during the entire evolution. Condensation occurs at low rates and only over the larger particles. As condensation proceeds, r* increases and fewer particles receive condensation. When these few particles become substantially larger, the collision of these particles with the smaller particles in the distribution becomes favored, and thus the larger particles become sinks for smaller particles. Thus, the larger particles grow due to preferential coagulation and preferential condensation.

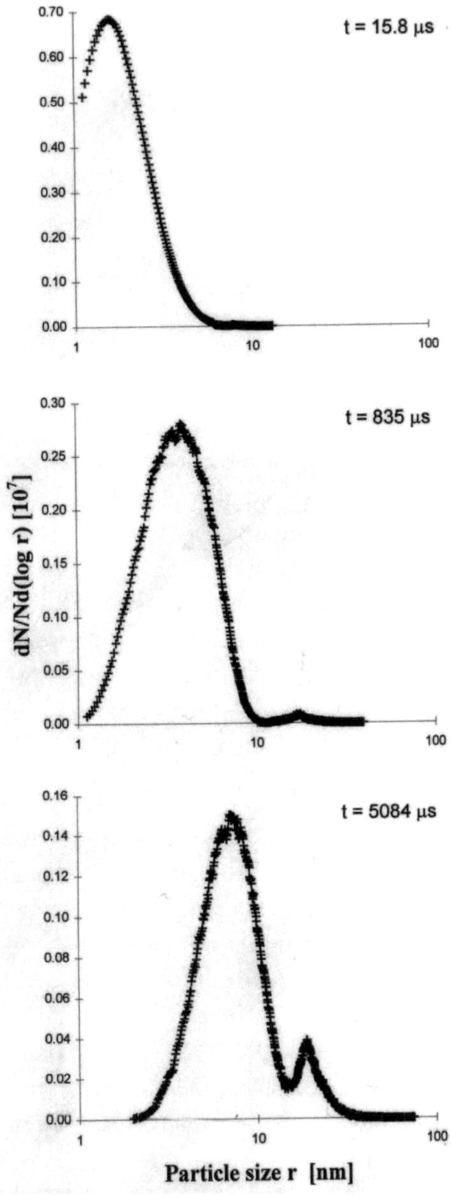

Figure 6. Evolution of an initially lognormal aerosol with S = 1.125, r_m = 1.86 nm, σ_g = 1.45, and N = 1.6 x 10^{19} ′particles/m^3 at constant temperature (1100°C).

3.1.1. Particle composition

Figure 8 shows the particle composition of the entire population after the first ms, i.e., after the bulk of the condensation has occurred (t = 5084 μs). The plot displays particle concentration

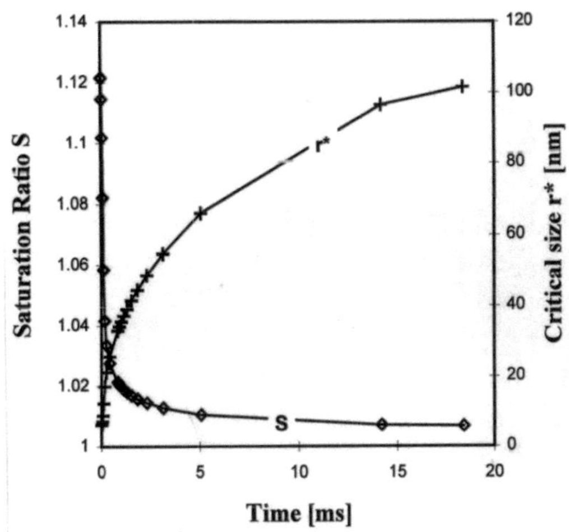

Figure 7. Evolution of S and r* for the conditions of Figure 6.

as a function of size for different compositions, and shows that composition is not a function of particle size, i.e., that for a given size there is not a unique composition. However, particles with similar composition remain grouped. For example, uncoated particles are grouped in the size range 2–12 nm. They constitute the majority of the population at this relatively early time. Thicker coatings are grouped in upper part of the distribution (r > 12 nm).

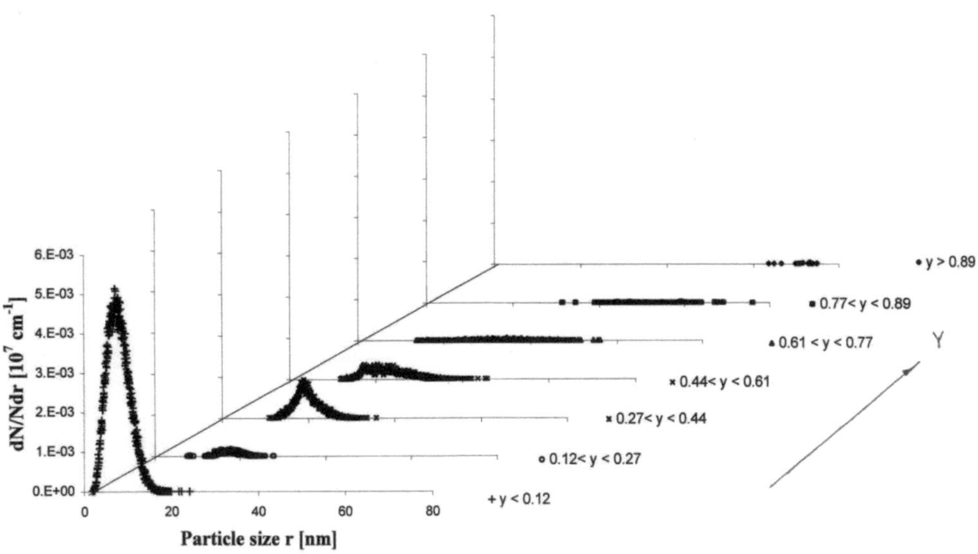

Figure 8. Particle composition for the conditions of Figure 6 at t = 5084 μs.

3.1.2. Core size distribution

The effect of the encapsulation process on the core size distribution can also be observed through the Markov-MC simulation. Figure 9 shows for the same conditions of Figure 6, the frozen and equilibrium core size distribution at 835 μs and 5084 μs, and compares them with the total particle size distribution. The frozen solution is characterized by a very high concentration of cores at $r \sim r_{mo}$ when the bulk of condensation has ceased. r_{mo} is the mean size of the particles at the onset of condensation. This is because with the frozen solution, the size of the uncoated particles is preserved when they collide with coated particles. The equilibrium core size distribution is similar to the particle size distribution when only coagulation occurs. However, the presence of the coating increases the *apparent* core size and the probability of collision of the coated particles increases. Consequently, the distribution has a higher concentration of particle for $r > r_m(t)$ compared to the lognormal distribution. Figure 9 also shows that the equilibrium core size distribution is unimodal, while the presence of the coating creates a bimodal distribution for the total particle size.

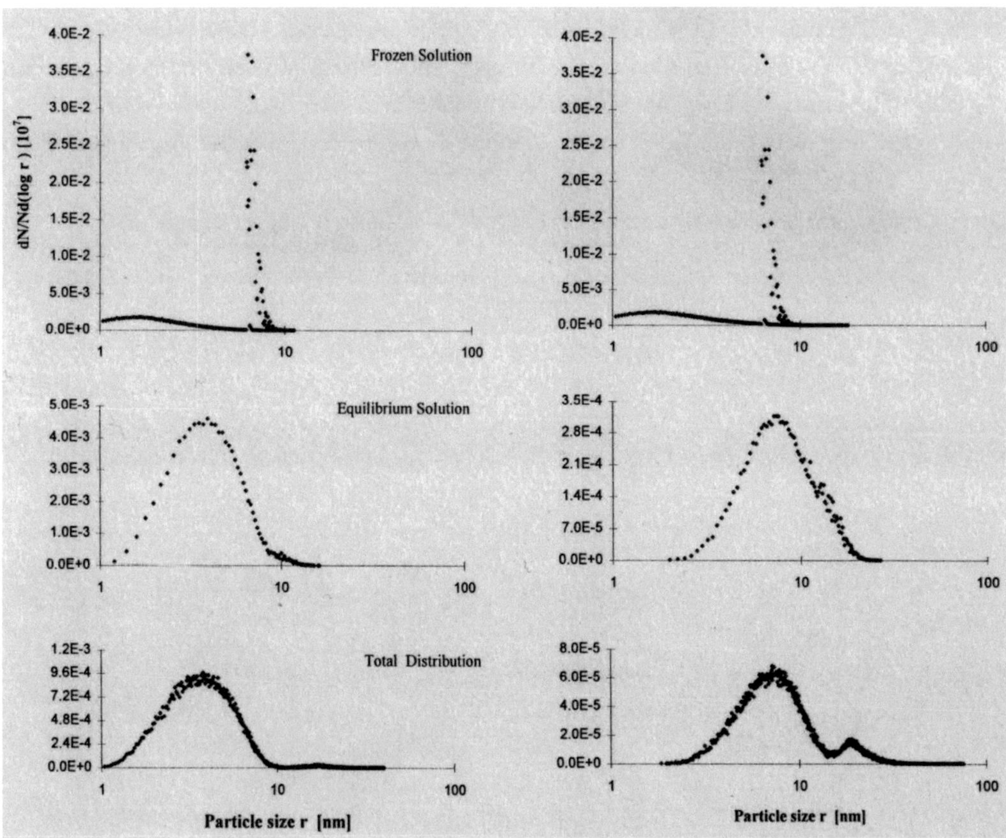

Figure 9. Frozen and equilibrium primary core size distribution for the conditions of Figure 6 at a) t = 835 μs and b) t = 5084 μs.

3.1.3. Evolution of a single tag particle

The Markov-MC simulation also allows the evolution of a single particle in the aerosol to be observed. Figure 10 shows the evolution of a typical particle in the aerosol (initial size r_o = 6 nm,). It shows that the particle grows by condensation (r^*_o = 5 nm) and coagulation up to r = 15.6 nm in 5 ms. The growing process involved 15 collisions. Figure 14 shows that during this time interval, the tag particle collides only with uncoated particles. It also shows that the amount of NaCl in the tag particle at the moment of collision is minor (y < 0.1).

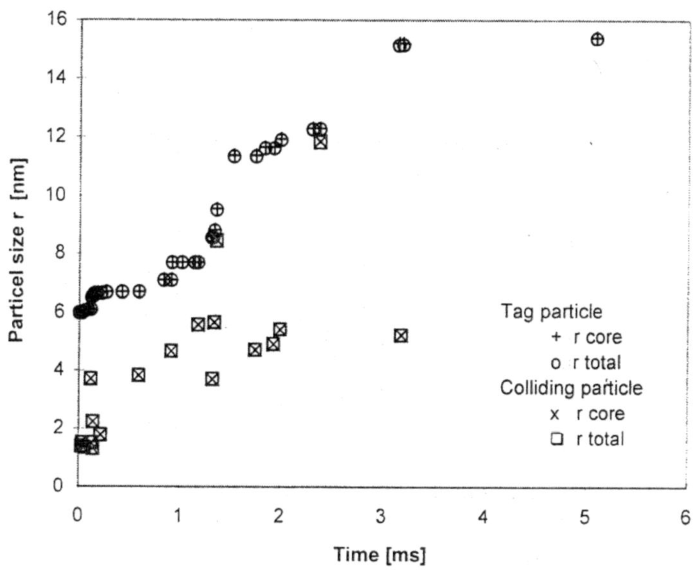

Figure 10. Evolution of a tag particle (r_o = 6 nm) during the encapsulation process for the conditions of Figure 6. "o" and "+" are the radii of the tag particle with and without NaCl encapsulation, respectively, at the moment of collision. "□" and "x" are the size of the colliding particles with and without NaCl encapsulation, respectively, at the moment of collision.

3.1.4. Discussion

The results obtained show that condensation is characterized by a very short initial high rate of condensation followed by a long period of slow condensation. For the conditions presented, the coated particles pose a light coating. The fraction of particles being coated can be estimated through the cumulative distribution function (F) by assuming that the particles prior to the onset of condensation are lognormally distributed. Figure 11 shows the fraction of particles in a lognormal distribution with size smaller than r/r_m. Thus, $1-F((r^*/r_m)_o)$ is the fraction of particles being coated. $(r^*/r_m)_o$ is the ratio of the critical particle size and mean particle size of the distribution at the onset of condensation. Therefore, for the conditions presented, only a small percentage of the population is coated directly.

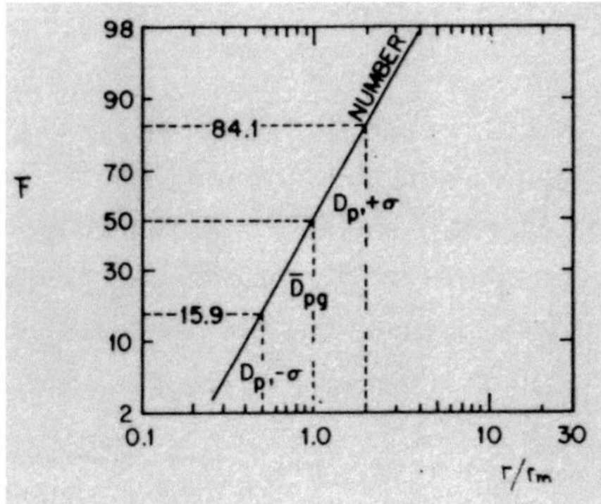

Figure 11. Number of particles in lognormal distribution with size smaller than $r_{/rm}$. 1- $F((r^*/r_m)_o)$ is the fraction of particles being coated for a given $(r^*/r_m)_o$ in an aerosol at constant temperature that experience an instantaneous change in the vapor-phase saturation conditions. $(r^*/r_m)_o$ is the ratio of the critical particle size and mean particle size of the distribution at the onset of condensation. (From Reference 64)

Allowing the aerosol to evolve further would result in collisions between coated and uncoated particles and would thus produce *encapsulated* particles. Nonetheless, it is useful to determine conditions where it is possible to directly coat a greater percentage of particles in the aerosol. Alternatively, we will consider conditions where the rate of particle growth due to coagulation is much higher than the rate of condensation, i.e., conditions for S(T) and N(t) are sought such that the rate of growth of r_m is higher than the rate of growth of r*. The rate of growth of r_m is proportional $1/\tau_{coll}$, while the rate of growth of r* is proportional to N/τ_{cond}. Table 4 shows values for τ_{cond} and τ_{coll} for a Ti/NaCl/Ar aerosol at 1100°C. From here, it can be concluded that for these conditions, the rate of condensation is much higher than the rate of coagulation, at least initially, when S is relatively large.

S	r* [nm]	N_0 [Particles/m^3]	τ_{coll} [μs]	τ_{cond} [μs]
1.200	3.8	5.08×10^{18}	214	20.4
1.125	5.9	1.29×10^{18}	674	51.9
1.048	15.0	7.55×10^{16}	730	354

Table 4. $TiCl_4 + 4Na + aAr \rightarrow 4NaCl + Ti + aAr$. 1100°C

Equation 1 and Table 1, from Chapter 4, show that the rate of growth of r_m increases with N and $T^{1/2}$. However, the rate of growth of r* also increases with N and (P-Ps)/ $T^{1/2}$. Therefore, this analysis shows that for high values of S (S > 1.1), the rate of growth of r* is many orders of magnitude higher than the rate of growth of r_m. At higher temperatures, direct coating is more effective. Nonetheless, the extent of this improvement is minor. At higher temperatures, the amount of available condensable material is small and only a very light coating thickness can be obtained.

In principle, it might be possible to exploit the very fast rate of bulk condensation and rapidly coat most of the particles by suddenly increasing S so that $r^* \ll r_m$. The desire effect might be obtained by dropping the temperature of the aerosol instantaneously, (e.g., by passing the aerosol through a wave expansion) or by sweeping the aerosol in a region of high NaCl concentration. In practice, the extremely high number densities in flames ($N \sim 10^{18}$ particles/m^3) make this process impractical because the timescale for coating is microseconds. Thus, the step change in S would have to occur on a submicrosecond timescale.

3.2. Encapsulation at constant heat loss

The results for a constant temperature aerosol have demonstrated a number of observations that are essential toward understanding nano-encapsulation in flames or other aerosols with similar high number densities. The most important observation is that because of the high number density, condensation is extremely fast even if only the tail of the size distribution is coated. Since r* grows as S decreases, the largest particles receive most of the subsequent coating and smaller particles remain uncoated, until they collide with the larger coated particles. Furthermore, since for condensation to occur, S = 1 is the lowest value of S, in constant temperature aerosols most of the condensable material will remain indefinitely as vapor, i.e., S = 1 at the flame temperature gives the lowest possible vapor pressure.

In practice, the environment downstream the flame zone is not at constant temperature. Radiative and convective heat loss can result in substantial heat loss from the aerosol. Heat loss potentially is quite beneficial to nano-encapsulation as can be understood by considering the two concerns discussed above when temperature is constant. First with heat loss, r* reduces as temperature decreases. This will allow more particles to be directly coated. Second, with the resulting decrease in temperature, virtually all the condensable vapor will eventually condense out.

Initially, the aerosol is assumed to consist of a normal distribution of pure Ti particles embedded in a saturated gas-phase mixture of NaCl (S = 1.0) at 1100°C. This would be consistent with the conditions expected at the flame front for the experimental results in Chapter 2. The parameters of the distribution are assumed to be $r_m = 2.5$ nm and $\sigma = 0.4$. For these conditions, the total particle concentration is $N = 10^{18}$ particles/m^3.

For the same aerosol mass, several runs were made to study the effect of the initial distribution and the choice of this size on the evolution of the aerosol. The characteristics of the evolution of an aerosol subject to pure coagulation were discussed in Chapter 4, and therefore will be omitted here, but the key observation was that the aerosol distribution quickly evolves to a distribution that is not a function of the initial size distribution.

The time required for a coagulating aerosol to reach a given r_m can be estimated by Markov-MC simulating the evolution of an initially monodisperse aerosol. Figure 12 shows the evolution of r_m as coagulation occurs. It also shows the reduction in the particle concentration during coagulation. Figure 12 has been nondimensionalized such that it is independent of the physical properties of the aerosol; however, it is limited to aerosol in the FMR.

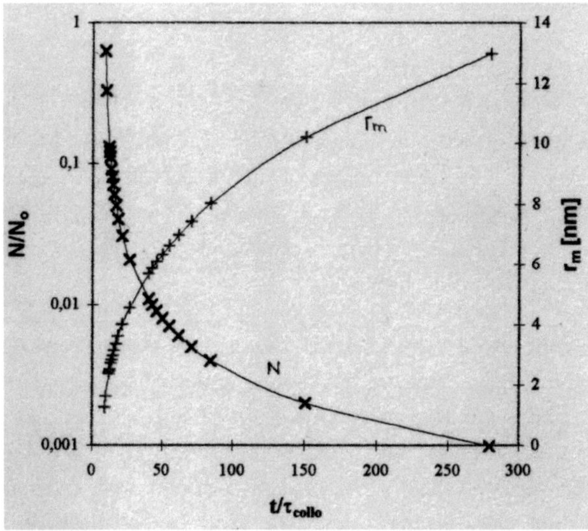

Figure 12. Time required for an initially monodisperse coagulating aerosol to reach a given r_m as simulated by the Markov-MC model.

The outputs from pure coagulation were taken as the initial conditions just prior to condensation, and the evolution of the aerosol subject to heat loss was observed. Figure 13 shows the evolution of the aerosol when the initial mean size is r_m~25 nm and the rate of heat loss is 10^{-6} W/m^3. Heat loss of 10^{-6} W/m^3 is high but reasonable for these heavily particle-laden flames. As temperature decreases, the vapor becomes supersaturated and condensation occurs over the large particles in the aerosol. Initially, the rate of bulk condensation is smaller than the rate of cooling. Therefore, as seen in Figure 14, S increases, r* decreases, and the number of particles receiving condensation increases. As the number of particles being encapsulated increases, the cooling process is retarded by the increase in the latent heat release. Soon a balance between the rate of heat loss and the bulk condensation rate is established. S approaches a maximum and r* a minimum. This minimum determines the percentage of the particles being coated. When the aerosol temperature approaches the melting point of the condensable material, the saturation pressure curve of the condensable material becomes less steep (see Figure 2) and the inverse process occurs. S becomes smaller and r* larger. The code was stopped at 100 ms as all the NaCl had condensed o_ut by this time.

The net effect on the particle size distribution and particle composition is shown in Figure 13. For the conditions and times of this simulation, condensation and coagulation are equally important (τ_{cond}~τ_{coll}). At the early stages, the interaction of coagulation and condensation creates small perturbations in the tail of the particle size distribution. The perturbations could be created due to the changes in dr*/dt relative to dr_m/dt. Coagulation decreases the concentration of small particles and magnifies these perturbations, creating a characteristic pattern. For the initial conditions chosen a 4-modal distribution is created. When r* reaches its maximum, condensation persists only on a very small fraction of particles, creating a big gap between this fraction of large particles and the main distribution. Alternatively, the perturba-

http://dx.doi.org/10.5772/62019

tions could be an artifact of the Markov-MC model. Several runs were made varying the type of grid, number of sections per unit length, and number of parcels. In all the cases, the same pattern was obtained. Further studies are required to understand the nature of these characteristic patterns.

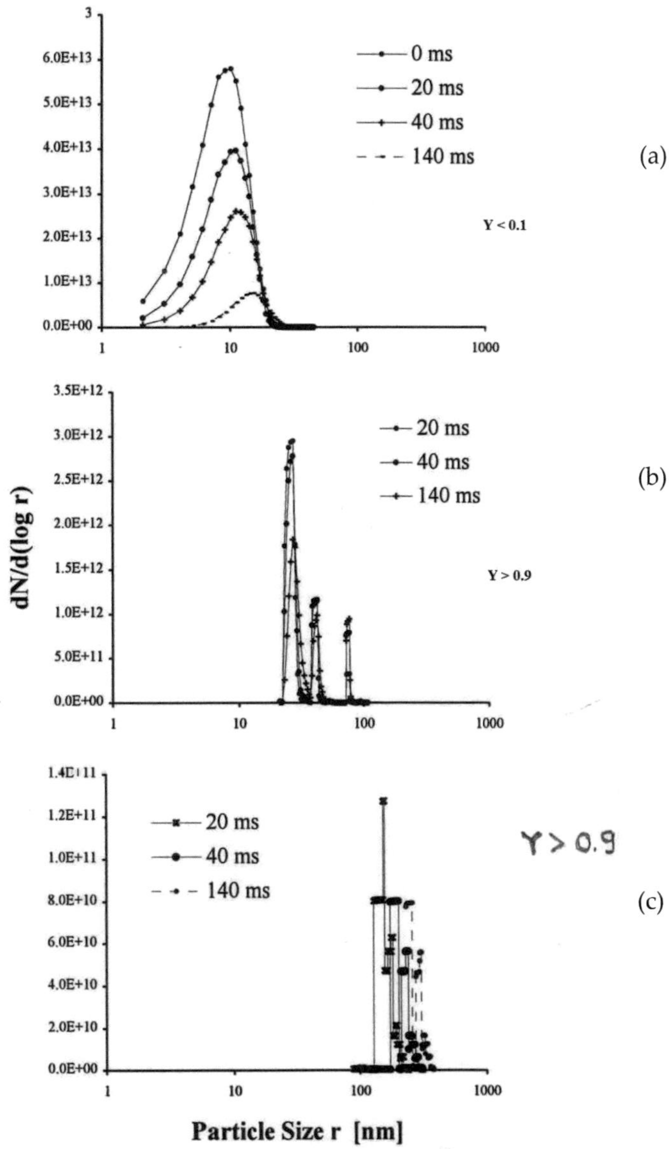

Figure 13. Evolution of particles with (a) Y < 0.1, (b) 0.1 < Y < 0.925, and (c) Y > 0.925 in a Ti/NaCl/Ar aerosol initially at 1100°C with r_m = 25 nm, S = 1.0, and N1.38 x 10^{15} particles/m^3, subject to heat loss of 10^{-6}W/m^3. The initial distribution is the one obtained after coagulation of the aerosol, starting from a normal distribution with r_m = 2.5nm, and N = 1.0 x 10^{18} particles/m^3.

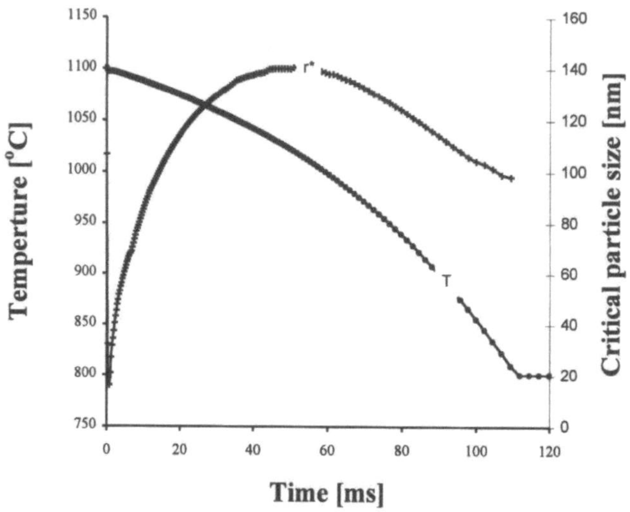

Figure 14. Evolution of r* and T during condensation at constant heat loss for the conditions of Figure 13.

The results show that by cooling the aerosol at rather high but realistic rates, only a fraction of the particles in the aerosol are initially coated and these particles contain most of the condensable material. The following discussion evaluates conditions for coating a greater fraction of particles when the aerosol is subject to constant heat loss.

Neglecting the Kelvin effect, the rate of condensation in the FMR is only a function of temperature and the physical properties of the condensable material. Therefore, for a given mass of aerosol and a given heat loss rate, the fraction of particles being encapsulated depends on particle concentration. The mean size of the core particles for a given N is determined by mass conservation.

To maximize the number of particles initially coated, values of N that make S a maximum but are below S_{crit} during the cooling process are sought. High values of N increase the rate of bulk condensation since the surface area for condensation increases. Thus, the concentration of condensable material rapidly decreases. Furthermore, the latent heat release retards the cooling process and consequently the rate of increase of S. Both processes force S to quickly approach unity, which leads to a low fraction of particles being encapsulated.

For low values of N, particle size increases but the surface area for condensation is smaller. Since the latent heat release is similar in both cases (because there is a balance between heat loss and condensation rate), the number of particles initially coated is approximately the same but the percentage of the particles being coated is greater in this case.

Several simulations were performed to establish a relationship between N and the percentage of particles initially coated and the results are shown in Table 5. These results were obtained for the same initial conditions as for Figure 13.

Rm[nm]	N[particles/m³]	% initially coated particles
2.5	1.38E+18	0.5
5.0	1.18E+17	1.7
10	2.39E+16	6.7
25	1.53E+15	20.0
50	1.91E+14	81.0

Table 5. Relationship between N and the percentage of coated particles during 100 ms for an aerosol initially at 1100°C and S = 1.0 subject to heat loss of 10^{-6} W/m³.

Table 5 shows for this rate of heat dissipation, most of the particles can be encapsulated when the particle concentration is low, i.e., when the particles are large. Since the percentage of coated particles for a given N is a weak function of the particle size, it is possible to have high percentage of encapsulation with particles of smaller size by controlling the concentration of the reactants such that N~10^{14} particles/m³ for the desired value of r_m. However, this limits the production rates and requires high levels of reactant dilution for small core particle sizes.

3.2.1. *Coagulation after condensation*

When the aerosol temperature is significantly below T_{sat}, the condensable vapor has been depleted, condensation ceases, and coagulation after condensation is the dominant process. During this time period, indirect encapsulation of the particles occurs via coagulation of the coated particles with the uncoated particles. To study this process, the results from the previous runs were taken as initial conditions, and the evolution of the aerosol was observed. Temperature was held constant at 800°C. Figure 15 shows the evolution of the aerosol for different particle compositions. Initially, most of the particles have composition Y < 0.1. Preferential coagulation of the large, heavily coated particles (Y > 0.92) with the small uncoated particles occur ($Z \sim \beta_{ij} N_i N_j$ and β_{ij} is the greatest for the combination of large and small particles) and therefore the uncoated particles become encapsulated within the coated particles. Middle size particles begin to coagulate when the concentration of small particles has decreased (small-middle size particles first and large-middle size particles later). Coagulation fills out the gaps in the particle size distribution. Eventually, all the particles in the aerosol will collide with the large heavily coated particles. The concentration and size of the large particles remains approximately constant during the coagulation process. A very large number of small particles are required to change their size significantly. Therefore, particle size and concentration after long times can be estimated by the size and concentration of this group of large particles. Figure 15 shows that for the conditions chosen, the final NaCl particle size is r_f~300 nm and the final concentration is N_f~10^{14} particles/m³. Experimental observation indicates that the final NaCl particle size is ~150 nm.

Considering the frozen solution, Figure 16 shows the percentage of particles being encapsulated as a function of time. It shows an exponential behavior with 90% of the particles being encapsulated within the first ~600 ms. This shows that coagulation after condensation ensures that most of the particles are encapsulated within a time period comparable to the typical experimental residence times(>1 s).

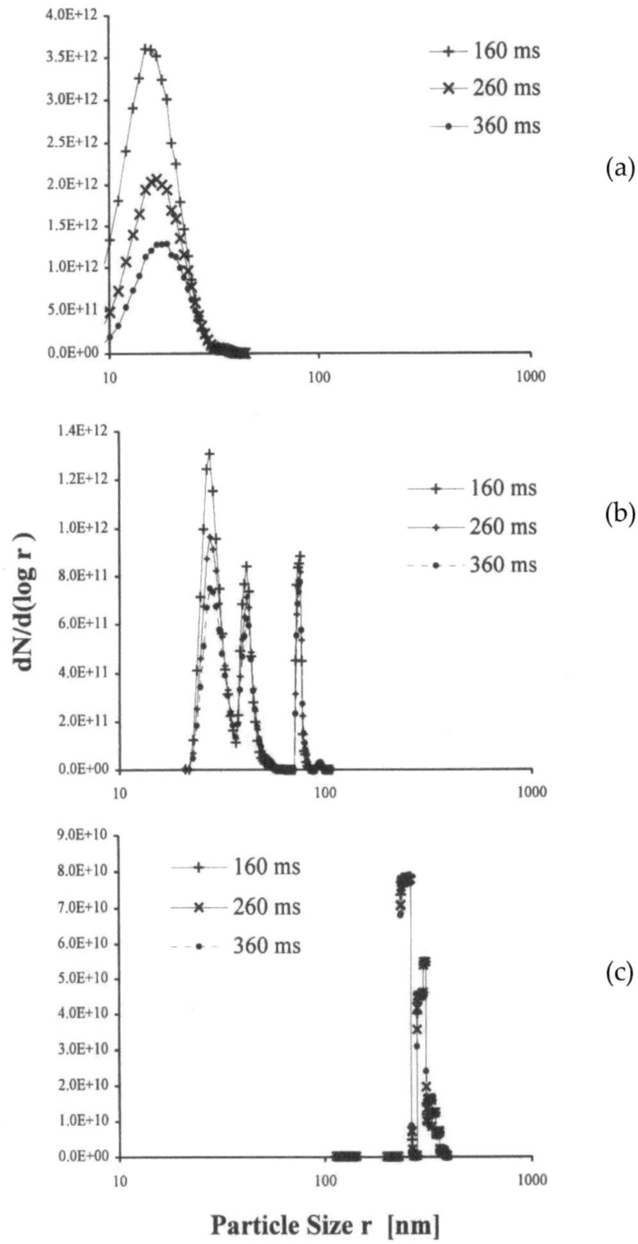

Figure 15. Evolution of the aerosol as function of particle composition with composition (a) $Y < 0.1$, (b) $0.1 < Y < 0.925$, and (c) $Y > 0.925$ at t = 160, 260, and 360 ms after condensation has been completed for the conditions of Figure 13. Temperature was held constant at 800°C.

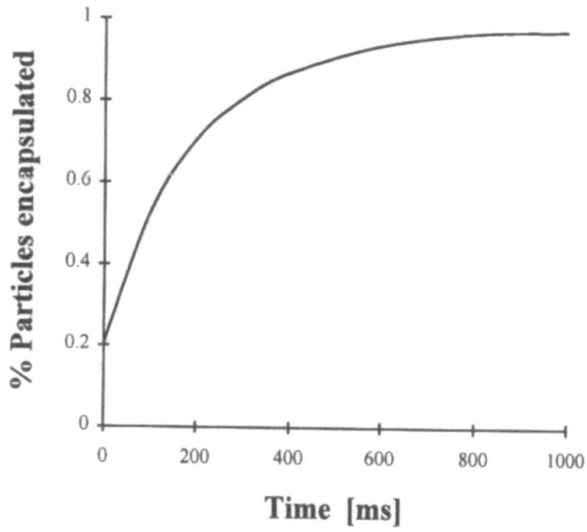

Figure 16. Percentage of particles being encapsulated via coagulation of the uncoated particles with the coated particles for the conditions of Figure 15.

3.2.2. Discussion

The results of the numerical simulation do not predict the concentration and size of the core particles. However, they can be estimated as follows: According to Table 5 and Figure 15, ~10^{14} NaCl particles/m^3 of size r~300 nm are formed by the time that most of the Ti particles have been encapsulated. Assuming that the mean size of the Ti particles at the beginning of the cooling process is r_m~25 nm, Table 5 predicts that ~20% of the 10^{15} particles/m^3 are coated at the end of the condensation process. Therefore, during the subsequent coagulation process, in average each coated particle coagulates with 5 uncoated particles, and these 6 core particles will coagulate within the NaCl matrix (see section 6.2.1). Therefore, the final size of the particle is ~$5^{1/3}$ r_m = 43 nm. Experimental results show 35 nm single core Ti particles within a NaCl droplet of ~150 nm (see Figure 9, Chapter 9). Approximately 10 AlN particles of size 24 nm within a NaCl particle[43] have been observed. This is expected since, for 24 nm there are ~10^{15} particles/m^3 and therefore for the same final number of NaCl particles there must be ~10 particles per NaCl particle.

Furthermore TiB_2 results show ~100 nm NaCl particles with hundreds of r~3–6 nm TiB_2 particles.[26] Again, this is expected since for the same final number of NaCl particles there are 100–1000 more 3–6 nm TiB_2 particles. The previous results show qualitative agreement with experimental results. This demonstrates the ability of the Markov-MC model to simulate particle dynamics in two-component aerosols.

4. Summary

A phenomenological description of the particle encapsulation method observed in sodium/halide flames has been presented and the Markov-MC model has been used to study the evolution of an M/NaCl/Ar combustion aerosol. Nano-encapsulation is obtained directly by condensing the second phase material (NaCl) over the M core particles, producing coated particles, and indirectly via coagulation of the uncoated particles with coated particles. Direct encapsulation occurs through heterogeneous condensation of supersaturated vapors.

Particle encapsulation at constant temperature was studied. The results are characterized by a very short initial high rate of condensation followed by a long period of slow rate of condensation. Only a very small percentage of the population is coated, and the encapsulated particles possess a very light coating. The alternatives to increase the number of particles being encapsulated and the thickness of the encapsulation are not practical or feasible. Encapsulation when the aerosol is subject to constant heat loss was studied. This process exploits the facts that by dropping aerosol temperature more condensable material is available for encapsulation and more particles are directly encapsulated since r^* obtain lower values. Results show that only a small fraction of the particles receive most of the condensable material. The concentration and size of these particles determine the final size and concentration of the NaCl particles. Conditions to encapsulate most of the particles during the cooling process were sought. It was found that for the same mass of aerosol, the percentage of coated particles can be increased by decreasing particle concentration. Encapsulation of uncoated particles via coagulation with the coated particles was also studied. Results show that 90% of the particles can be encapsulated within a time period comparable to the typical experimental residence time. Numerical results for particle size and number of particles within a NaCl particle show good agreement with experimental observations for Ti, AlN, and TiB_2. This work has gained substantial understanding in the particle encapsulation process and has shown the usefulness of the Markov-MC model to study two-component aerosols.

Author details

Jose Ignacio Huertas

Address all correspondence to: jhuertas@itesm.mx

Tecnológico de Monterrey, Mexico

Section 7

Conclusions

Chapter 7

Conclusions and Recommendations

Jose Ignacio Huertas

Additional information is available at the end of the chapter

http://dx.doi.org/10.5772/62018

Flame synthesis is a very attractive route for industrial production of nanophase materials. However, contamination and agglomeration of the starting particles are serious drawbacks for this technique. These problems are addressed in this work by using the particle encapsulation method originally proposed by Axelbaum, et al.[26] The basic approach of the particle encapsulation process is to allow the nucleation and growth of the primary particles to proceed normally but then coat these particles, with an appropriate material, when they have grown to the required size and before they begin to agglomerate, thus producing encapsulated particles. These particles will agglomerate, but the primary particles within them will not. When the coating is later removed, the resulting powder will contain only weakly agglomerated particles. During subsequent handling, the encapsulation protects air-sensitive nanophase particles like W and Ti from oxidation or contamination.

This work has demonstrated the use of the encapsulation method by synthesizing unagglomerated nonoxide tungsten (W) and tungsten titanium (W-Ti) nanosized particles in a sodium/halide flame. This work also has provided substantial insight into understanding the encapsulation process by numerically simulating the dynamics of particle formation in combustion aerosols through the Markov-MC method developed in this work as well. The Markov-MC method is a general technique to simulate particle dynamics in two-component aerosol subject to simultaneous nucleation, condensation, and coagulation. A summary of the main conclusions obtained during the development of this work follows.

1. Synthesis of nanosized W, Ti, and W-Ti particles by flame synthesis

High-quality nanosized W, Ti, and W-Ti nanoparticulates were produced and consolidated to demonstrate the applicability of the flame synthesis process to produce nanosized materials and of the encapsulation method to control purity and agglomeration of nanosized particles.

Nanoparticulates of W, Ti, and W-Ti were synthesized by a gas-phase combustion process employing exchange reactions between sodium and metal chlorides. The sodium/halide chemistry is exothermic and has thermodynamic yields of 100% for T < 1250°C. To minimize agglomeration and protect the particles from contamination during subsequent exposure to atmosphere, the NaCl by-product was condensed onto the particles within the flame. Gaseous reactants were introduced into an open atmosphere burner forming a coflow diffusion-flame. Several runs were made to optimize the characteristics of the produced powder.

The collected powders were characterized by X-ray diffraction (XRD), scanning electron microscopy (SEM), and transmission electron microscopy (TEM). XRD was used for phase identification of bulk powder samples and to obtain information about the size of the nano-crystallites using the X-ray line broadening method (i.e., the Scherrer formula). SEM and TEM studies of the powders were carried out to determine particle size. Elemental composition was determined by energy disperse X-ray analysis (EDAX). Powders were exposed to atmosphere and XRD characterization studies were performed in open atmosphere.

Nanocrystalline W particles were produced by reacting Na and WCl_6. The W particles appear unagglomerated, cubic and hexagonal in shape, and have an average size of ca. 30 nm. XRD results indicate the presence of only α-W, β-W, and NaCl. No contamination is detected even after extended exposure to atmospheric conditions. Vacuum heat treatment of the powders at 800°C results in effective removal of NaCl with no detectable change in particle size. The heat treatment also transforms the β-W phase to α-W.

A nanopowder consisting of W-Ti was also produced via Na/WCl_6/$TiCl_4$ chemistry. XRD spectra of as-produced powders show only W and NaCl. EDAX indicates the presence of Ti, and analysis of lattice parameters suggests that part, not all, of the Ti is in solid solution. Particles are unagglomerated, cubic in shape, with an average size of ca. 30 nm. Heat treating the sample at 850°C increases average particle size to ca. 40 nm. When the amount of Ti is increased to 22 wt%, XRD spectra of as-produced powders show small peaks of α-Ti and β-Ti, in addition to W and NaCl.

The nanocrystalline W and W-Ti powders were successfully consolidated into pellets of 6 mm diameter and 6–8 mm long. Densities as high as 97% were achieved by hot pressing and hipping at temperatures of $0.42T_m$ to $0.48T_m$. Microstructures of the consolidates consist of nanometer-sized grains (40 nm). Hardness measurements indicate hardness values 4 times that of conventional tungsten.

To investigate the effectiveness of different methods of removing the NaCl from the as-produced samples, heat-treated and water-wash samples were analyzed for Na and Cl. Na was determined by ICP-atomic emission spectroscopy and Cl by ion chromatography. When the sample was heat treated at 850°C for 10 h, results showed 0.025 wt% residual Na and 0.02 wt% residual Cl, indicating that the salt encapsulation can be effectively removed. Similar elemental analysis tests have shown the effectiveness of the NaCl encapsulation method protecting the powder from contamination. AlN was synthesized with an 0_2 content <0.8 wt %, while traditional methods offer AlN with oxygen content >5 wt%.

2. Monte Carlo simulation of two-component aerosol processes

To gain insight into the understanding of the particle encapsulation method, a code to simulate particle formation in two-component aerosols has been developed. The simulation is carried out using a Monte Carlo technique. This approach allows for the combination of probabilistic and deterministic events. Thus, the nonlinear terms of the general dynamic equation (GDE) were Monte Carlo simulated, and the other more workable terms were solved analytically and incorporated into the model. To simulate coagulation, a uniform mixture was assumed and only collisions were simulated, not in the physical sense but as a transition in a Markov chain. The model includes nucleation, condensation, coagulation, sources, and sinks for two-component aerosol processes. The Kelvin effect and particle heating due to condensation have been included in the model as well.

The code is general and does not suffer from problems associated with numerical dispersion, mass conservation, and approximations on particle composition. It has been validated for the case of constant temperature, constant collision frequency, and initially monodisperse aerosols where only coagulation is important and where there is an analytical solution to the GDE. Table 1 compares the Markov-Monte Carlo (Markov-MC) method with the sectional method. From here it can be concluded that the Markov-MC method offers important advantages and is an attractive tool to study particle dynamics in two-component aerosols.

Method	Markov-MC	Sectional
Solution	Probabilistic Simulate collisions as a transition is a Markov chain. Nucleation and condensation are solved analytically and couple with coagulation through time.	Deterministic Solve m ODEs, where m is the number of sections
Assumptions	Within a size-composition section, particles assume same dynamic mean size and same dynamic mean composition	Within a size section, particles have same constant size and constant composition
Best application	Very short timescales Combustion aerosols	Very large timescales Atmospheric aerosols
Relative Advantages	• Higher resolution in size and time • Easy to incorporate new phenomena	• Deterministic solution
Weaknesses	• Probabilistic approach	• Numerical diffusion • Problems associated with mass conservation • Problems handling simultaneous condensation and coagulation

Table 1. Comparison of the Markov-MC and Sectional numerical methods.

3. Numerical simulation of the particle encapsulation process

The Markov-MC method was applied to M/NaCl/Ar combustion aerosols to study the particle encapsulation process. This type of aerosol is formed during the production of nanosized powders in sodium/halide flames and is composed of M, NaCl, and Ar, where M is a metal or ceramic. The aerosol is characterized by very high particle concentrations (~10^{18} particles/m^3) and high temperatures (>1000°C). Furthermore, the M/NaCl/Ar aerosol is a two-component aerosol, since both M and NaCl are condensable phases.

Particle formation in flames is affected by many factors that make a complete analysis of this process extremely complicated. Particle dynamics, chemical kinetics, heat and mass transfer fields are some of the factors that affect the final product. Despite these complications, considerable insight was gained by focusing attention on aerosol dynamics alone and considering the burner as an idealized plug flow reactor in which the relevant gas-phase chemistry and transport are decoupled from the particle dynamics. This can be done since the characteristics of the final particles, for example, size distribution and morphology, are primarily affected by coagulation and condensation, i.e., by aerosol dynamics.

Particle dynamics in M/NaCl/Ar aerosols involves the formation and growth of M and NaCl particles by nucleation, condensation, and coagulation. Since NaCl is the more volatile material, encapsulation of M particles occurs, either directly when the NaCl vapor condenses onto the M particles producing NaCl-coated M particles, or indirectly when uncoated particles coagulate with the coated particles. Since the encapsulation process is not directly affected by nucleation of M, it was assumed that nucleation and condensation of M has been completed before the onset of NaCl condensation. An initial size distribution for M was assumed, and the evolution of the aerosol subject to coagulation and condensation was modeled. The modeling reduced to solving the governing equation through the Markov-MC model under appropriate assumptions and conditions. The main assumptions and conditions are about the morphology of the particles, the effect of temperature during the condensation process, and the working regime.

3.1. Particle spheroidicity

Particle sintering is a strong function of particles size and temperature. It was found that for 800°C < T < 1400°C, Ti and W particles smaller than ~50 nm in radii sinter within a period of time much shorter than the shortest scale in the process. Then sintering can be assumed instantaneous and particles spheroidicity at any time during the simulation. Based on this results, particles were assumed to be made of a M core coated with NaCl.

3.2. Constant temperature during condensation

A heat transfer model was developed to evaluate the increase in particle temperature and gas-phase temperature due to latent heat release during NaCl condensation. It was shown that for the CR the increase in particle temperature is negligible, but in the FMR it is substantial. For NaCl condensation at 1100°C it was found that the increase in temperature is upto ~37°C for

S = 1.5. Furthermore, it was found that the rate of condensation when particle heating effects are included is about 4 times less than when particle temperature is assumed constant. These heating effects were included in the model.

3.3. Working regime

For typical experimental conditions of M/NaCl/Ar aerosols, 0.01 < Kn < 10.0. Therefore, the well-known Fuchs-Sutugin correction factor for condensation and coagulation in the transition regime was included. Implementation of more accurate correlation of more accurate correlation is straightforward.

This study was intended to allow for an understanding of the dominant mechanism involved in the nano-encapsulation process and to demonstrate the usefulness of the model in studying two-component aerosols. Two cases were considered: constant temperature and constant heat loss. The constant temperature case was considered to introduce the salient features of nano-encapsulation, nonetheless, heat loss which is intrinsic to most flame systems, was shown to be of fundamental importance in controlling nano-encapsulation.

The results were not expected to yield quantitative agreement with experiments because the flame has a complex 2D structure and the aerosol was assumed to be uniform and evolving with time. Nonetheless, we expect the model to elucidate the essential features of nano-encapsulation. The system of Ti through the Na/Cl/Ti/Ar chemistry was used as a case study.

3.3.1. Encapsulation at constant temperature

The constant temperature condition applies to very diluted aerosols or to systems where the rate of latent heat release can be dissipated as it is generated. As an initial study, a case where a sudden encapsulation occurs in the preexisting aerosol was considered. The aerosol is subjected to a step change in saturation ratio as might be experienced in flames, expansion shock waves, mixing, or sudden drops in temperature. The main characteristic of the evolution of the aerosol is that because of the high number density, condensation is extremely fast and only a small fraction of the tail of the size distribution is coated. Since r^* grows as S decreases, the largest particles receive most of the subsequent coating and smaller particles remain uncoated, until they collide with coated particles. Better conditions for encapsulating the particles are obtained when both the time prior to the onset of heterogeneous condensation and the drop temperature are maximized. Maximizing the time prior to condensation, coagulation ensures larger particles and lower particle concentration. Maximizing the drop in temperature, the mass vapor available for encapsulation increases. The combined conditions seek to maximize the mass of condensable material per particle in the aerosol. The upper limits for these time and drop in temperature are the onset of formation of agglomerated structures and the onset of homogeneous nucleation, respectively. However, the extremely high number densities in flames ($N{\sim}1O^{18}$ particles/m^3) make this process impractical because the timescale for coating is microseconds. Thus, the step change in T would have to occur on a submicrosecond timescale.

Another drawback of this encapsulation alternative is that it only uses a small fraction (100(S-1)%) of the entire mass of the condensable material to encapsulate the particles. Since for condensation to occur, S = l is the lowest value of S, in constant temperature aerosols, most of the condensable material remains indefinitely as vapor, i.e., S = l at the flame temperature gives the lowest possible vapor pressure. The total mass of the condensable material can be used to encapsulate the particles by controlling the rate of cooling of the aerosol such that only heterogeneous condensation occurs during the entire process.

3.3.2. *Encapsulation at constant heat loss*

In practice, the environment downstream the flame zone is not at constant temperature. Radiative and convective heat loss can result in substantial heat loss from the aerosol. Heat loss is quite beneficial to nano-encapsulation as can be understood by considering the two concerns discussed above when temperature is constant. First with heat loss, r* reduces as temperature reduces. This allows more particles to be directly coated. Second, with the resulting decrease in temperature, virtually all the condensable vapor eventually condense out. Several outputs from pure coagulation were taken as the initial conditions just prior to condensation, and the evolution of the aerosol subject to heat loss was observed. A rate of heat loss of 10^{-6} W/m^3 was used. Heat loss of 10^{-6} W/m^3 is high but reasonable for these heavily particle-laden flames. The results show that by cooling the aerosol, a fraction of the particles in the aerosol are initially coated and a small fraction of these particles contain most of the condensable material. For a given mass of aerosol and a given heat loss rate, the number of particles initially coated is maximized by decreasing N. When N decreases, particle size increases but the surface area for condensation is smaller. Since the latent heat release is the same, the number of particles initially coated is approximately the same. However, the percentage of the particles being coated increases. For any desired value of $r_{m,}$ ~80% of the particles are initially coated by controlling the concentration of the reactants such that N~10^{14} particles/m^3 for the chosen r_m. However, this alternative limits the production rate and requires high levels of reactant dilution for small core particle size. Greater percentage of coated particles can be obtained by increasing the rate of heat loss. This alternative, however, has physical constrains, and therefore is not feasible.

When the condensable vapor has been depleted, condensation ceases, and coagulation after condensation is the dominant process. During this time period, indirect encapsulation of the particles occurs via coagulation of the coated particles with the uncoated particles. The results from previous runs were taken as initial conditions, and the evolution of the aerosols was observed. Temperature was held constant at 800°C. Results show that the number of particles being encapsulated as a function of time has an exponential behavior with 90% of the particles being encapsulated within the first ~400 ms. This shows that coagulation after condensation ensures that most of the particles are encapsulated within a time period comparable to the typical experimental residence times(>1 s).

Results for M/NaCl/Ar aerosols under typical experimental conditions showed ~10^{14} particles/m^3 of total size r~300 nm. Assuming that the particles within the NaCl matrix collide and sinter, as expected in the case of Ti, the core size obtained was r~45 nm. These results are in qualitative agreement with experimental results where it was obtained particles of total size r~150 nm with single cores of size r~35 nm. On the other hand, assuming that the particles within the NaCl matrix remain separate, the number of cores within the NaCl matrix depends on the particle mean size prior to condensation. For example, if the mean size is r~20 nm, every particle contains ~10 cores. This again is in qualitative agreement with experimental results for the case of AlN, where ~10 AlN particles of ~24 nm per NaCl particle have been observed. Similar agreement was found for the case of TiB_2, where it hundreds of Ti cores within every NaCl particle have been observed.

Only qualitative agreement has been found between the Markov-MC simulations and the experimental results due to the strong simplifications made, and the lack of accurate temperature and species concentrations profiles in sodium/halide flames. The main simplifications were introduced when a 1D problem was assumed and particle dynamics decoupled from chemistry and flow field. The results presented have shown the ability of the Markov-MC model to simulate particle dynamics in two-component aerosols and have provided insight into the understanding of the particle encapsulation process by exploring the different alternatives where the encapsulation process is feasible and the alternatives to optimize it.

4. Recommendations

Further work is required to address the following issues:

- W and W-Ti production rates.

A laboratory-scale laminar sodium/halide flame was used here to synthesize W and W-Ti nanoparticles. The production rates were ~2g/h. Further work is required to increase this production rate up to ~20 kg/h. This can be done by operating the reactor in turbulent regime. Operating in turbulent regime, the turbulence mixes the reactants uniformly and therefore the amount of excess Na required in laminar flames to ensure 100% yields can be reduced. Besides optimizing the use of raw materials, this approach will reduce the presence of Na in the products, and consequently the possibility of contamination of the primary particles. Na reacts with the water in the atmosphere to produce sodium hydroxide (NaOH), which dissolves the NaCl protective coating, leaving the primary particles directly exposed to atmospheric conditions. Furthermore, the flame temperature will be higher since the reactants are in proportions closer to stoichiometry. With higher temperatures, primary particles have longer times for coagulation prior to the onset of condensation, and therefore N will be smaller. This condition favors the number of particles being coated during the condensation process. Other potential advantages of this approach are the lower energy required per gram of primary material produced, and the presence of more uniform aerosols. However, since the high of turbulent flames is larger the laminar ones, it is required to protect the particles at the exit of the burner from atmospheric entrainment with long heated extensions. It is also advisable to operate the burner upside-down to alleviate the clogging at the exit of the burner.

- Mechanical properties of the W and W-Ti consolidates.

A complete evaluation of the mechanical properties – both at static and at high rates of deformation – are required. The results of this characterization will lead to optimizing the different steps during the production of these materials, and thus their properties. The mechanical properties at high strain rates of the consolidates can potentially be improved by using starting powder of smaller size. It is believed that when the grain size approaches 1O nm in diameter,the material reaches its maximum strength. In addition, the idea of mixing pure nanosized W with pure nanosized Ti in the right proportions instead of simply consolidating W-Ti nanosized powder could be explored. With this approach, during consolidation Ti will constitute the desired soft matrix for the embedded W nanosized grains. Ti will diffuse into the W grains forming a shell of W-Ti in the outside of the W grains. This structure seems to be better that having the Ti in solid solution uniformly within the W grains.

- Alternative to demonstrating the effectiveness of the NaCl coating.

During this work, the particle encapsulation process was proven to be effective in controlling agglomeration and protecting the nanosized powder from contamination. Another alternative to demonstrate the benefits of the encapsulation process is to produce, under the same conditions, a given material with and without NaCl encapsulation. This can be done by reacting the respective halide with hydrogen to produce HCl gas. Besides providing a base for comparison, this experiment will be illuminating about the morphology of the particles. For example, the size of the particles prior to agglomeration will be observed. It has been postulated that the size of the particles in agglomerated structures depends only on the physical properties of the material and not on the synthesis process. Furthermore, the effect of the encapsulation over the particle size distribution will also be observed.

- Interactions of the condensable material with the core material.

The effect of the interactions of the condensable material with the core material on the rate of condensation requires further studies. Situations where, for example, a metal is encapsulated within another metal or a ceramic could have very different behaviors to that described here for NaCl and Ti.

- Re-evaporation.

The Markov-MC mode1 requires to inc1ude evaporation processes. Even though this is a straightforward step, it has not been included yet. The rate of decrease in particle size during evaporation is given by [98]:

$$\frac{dr}{dt}=\frac{4DM}{Rr\rho}\left(\frac{P_{\infty}}{T_{\infty}}-\frac{P}{T}\right)\left(\frac{\lambda+r}{2r+5.33\left(\frac{\lambda^2}{2r}\right)+3.42\lambda}\right) \tag{1}$$

where r is the size of the partic1e, the subscript ∞ refers to conditions removed from the partic1e and the other variables are evaluated at the particle surface. The 1ast factor in Equation 1 corrects for diffusion in the transition regime. For volatile particles such as water or alcohol, a correction must be included for the cooling of the droplet due to rapid evaporation. This self-cooling effect reduces the droplet temperature and, consequently the partial pressure at the droplet surface. Equation 1 also needs to be corrected to include the Kelvin effect. It is anticipated that including re-evaporation processes, the results obtained during the development of this work would not be substantially different. The number of particles being coated during condensation will decrease and the coated particles will have heavier coatings.

- Problem associated with condensation.

As already observed, during condensation at constant heat loss, a 4-modal distribution was obtained. The presence of these four modes was attributed to the change in the rate of bulk condensation or to artifacts of the Markov-MC model. The issue remained unresolved even when the same results were obtained for higher resolutions and denser grids. Since the particle ordering principle as discussed earlier is followed by most of the combustion aerosols, a moving grid will resolve this issue. The advantages of the Markov-MC model will still prevail and the implementation of the moving grid for condensation coupled to the Monte Carlo simulation of coagulation is straightforward.

- Compatibility of the Markov-MC model with other codes.

The Markov-MC model has the potential of being incorporated into time step marching codes that model the fluid-dynamics and the chemistry of flames. The possibility of producing general (universal) solutions to the evolution of aerosols subject to coagulation and condensation needs to be explored, since this type of solution will greatly simplify the modeling of aerosols where the flow field, chemistry, and particle dynamics are simultaneously important.

- Application of the Markov-MC model to other aerosol problems.

During this work, the Markov-MC model has been applied to combustion aerosols, which are characterized by high number densities, high temperatures, and high rates of condensation. However, the Markov-MC model is general and can be used to study other aerosol problems. For example, the modeling of atmospheric aerosols is an important application where the model can be exploited.

- Optimization of the code.

Relatively little effort has been put into optimizing the Markov-MC code. Several subroutines can be improved to reduce the computational time. Furthermore, a methodology to improve the code efficiency can be generated, where coarse solutions are produced first and finer solutions later. This methodology provides an additional mechanism to ensure that the grid and statistics used during the simulation are enough for accurate solutions.

- Markov-MC simulation of particle encapsulation process.

Experimental validation of the results obtained by Markov-MC simulating the evolution of M/NaCl/Ar aerosols and the particle encapsulation process is required. This step has several complications because of the nature of the sodium/halide flames. The presence of sodium limits the use of the typical experimental optical tools to study flames. The high temperatures and the very high number densities in sodium/halide flames make the information obtained through the use of thermocouples and aerosol samplers of little relevance. Furthermore, the numerical results were obtained for the equivalent 1D plug flow reactor, while the laminar sodium/halide flame has complicated 2D flow field. However, a qualitative validation can be obtained by exploring extreme conditions. For example, maintaining the aerosol at constant high temperature for very long periods of time will provide information about the effect of NaCl coating on the particle size distribution and particle morphology. Having a very diluted aerosol will provide information about the effect of the number density on the fraction of particles that can be encapsulated.

Author details

Jose Ignacio Huertas

Address all correspondence to: jhuertas@itesm.mx

Tecnológico de Monterrey, Mexico

Section 8

Appendix

Chapter 8

Appendices

Jose Ignacio Huertas

Additional information is available at the end of the chapter

http://dx.doi.org/10.5772/62017

1. Appendix A

1.1. Heating Effects

The aim of this appendix is to study the heat transfer process occurring during condensation. The motivation for such study comes from the uncertainty in the applicability of the *growth laws* to the case of a supersaturated vapor condensing over very small particles. These growth laws obtained assuming constant temperature. However, when condensation takes place at very high rates, the latent heat released may increase the temperature of the particle by several degrees. Then, considering that

- the rate of condensation is proportional to the net difference in partial pressure of the condensing material in the environment and at the surface of the particle (P_∞-P_p);
- the partial pressure at the surface of the particle is equal to the saturation pressure of the vapor (P_p= P_s), when the Kelvin effect is neglected; and
- the saturation pressure has a very strong dependence with temperature ($P_s = a^*T^n$, where a and n are constants, n~11 for NaCl),

it can be concluded that any small change in particle temperature could affect the rate of particle growth substantially. Dealing with condensation in the CR, it is common to argue that the increase in temperature is negligible and then the respective growth laws can be used directly. However, the situation could be very different in the FMR.

A heat transfer model has been developed to evaluate the extent of particle heating during the process of condensation in both the CR and FMR.

The system is a uniform liquid phase spherical droplet embedded in a supersaturated vapor. The initial conditions are same temperature for particle and vapor, and particle size slightly greater than the critical size for condensation.

Since the vapor concentration profile near the particle approaches a steady-state condition before appreciable growth occurs, the steady-state diffusional flux may be used to calculate the particle growth rate. As growth proceeds hundreds of times slower than diffusion, the profile near the particle remains close to its steady-state value at all times, whereas the transient region propagates farther from the particle.

S	τ_D[s]	τ_{cond}[s]	τ_{HT}[s]	Biot	r*[nm]
1.010	2.05x10-10	2.71x10-3	2.71x10-3	2.47x10-2	70.1
1.125	1.47x10-12	1.74x10-5	1.73x10-10		5.92
1.500	1.24x10-13	1.10x10-6	1.46x10-11		1.72

$\tau_{HT} = r^2/\alpha_p$ Characteristic heat transfer time inside of the particle

$\tau_D = r^2/D$ Characteristic diffusion time of NaCl vapor in Ar

Table 1. Characteristic times for a Ti/NaCl/Ar aerosol at 1100°C.

An energy balance describes the effects of latent heat release by condensation at the particle surface. Heat conduction occurs toward both the particle interior and the exterior gas phase. The ratio of the characteristic times for conduction within the droplet and the characteristic time for heat transfer in the gas phase is known as the *Biot number,* which can also can be interpreted as the ratio of the respective thermal resistances. The Biot number provides a measure of the temperature drop in the droplet relative to the temperature difference between the droplet surface and the gas phase:

$$Bi = \frac{2hr}{k_p} \tag{1}$$

where h is the convective heat transfer coefficient, and k_p is the thermal conductivity of the particle. Table 1 shows values for the characteristic time for conduction within the droplet and the Biot number for several conditions of supersaturation. Table 1 shows that the Biot number is of the order of O.O1 for the NaCl droplet in Ar at high temperatures (T~1100°C).

For Bi << 1 the resistance to conduction within the solid is much less than the resistance to convection across the fluid boundary layer. Hence, it can be assumed that the temperature within the so1id is uniform at any given time.

Heat Transfer in the CR

With this assumption, the energy conservation equation for the liquid droplet system can be expressed as:

$$\frac{\rho H_v}{M}\frac{dv}{dt} = \frac{\rho v C_p}{M}\frac{dT}{dt} + hA\left(T - T_\infty\right) \tag{2}$$

http://dx.doi.org/10.5772/62017

where ϱ is the particle density, H_v is the latent heat of condensation, υ is the volume of the particle, C_p is the heat capacity of the particle, M is the molecular weight of NaCl, *h* is the convective heat transfer coefficient, and A is the particle surface area.

The term on the left of Equation (2) represents the latent heat released during condensation; The first term on the right represents the energy absorbed by the particle in increasing its temperature, and the second term represents the energy dissipated by convection.

For convective heat transfer of a single sphere with a stagnant environment, the Nusselt number is equal to 2, ($N_u = 2$). Hence, the convective heat transfer coefficient *h* is equal to the thermal conductivity of the gas (K_g), divided by the radii of the sphere $h=K_g/r$.

Nondimensionalizing particle size as $\eta=r/r^*$, where r* is critical size for condensation; temperature as $\Psi= (T-T\infty) / \zeta$ where $\zeta=3H_v/C_p$; and time as $\tau=t/\tau_{cond}$, the energy equation reduces to:

$$\frac{d\Psi}{d\tau}=\frac{1}{\eta}\frac{d\eta}{d\tau}-\xi_{CR}\frac{\Psi}{\eta^2} \quad (3)$$

where the parameter ξ_{CR} is given by:

$$\xi_{CR}=\frac{3MK_g\tau_{cond}}{\rho C_p r^{*2}} \quad (4)$$

The rate of growth equation for condensation in the CR in its nondimensional form is reprinted here for the reader's convenience:

$$\frac{d\eta}{d\tau}=\frac{1}{Ln(S)}\frac{1}{\eta}\left(1-S^{\frac{1}{\eta}-1}\right) \quad (5)$$

The energy equation and the growth rate equation need to be solved numerically, subject to the initial conditions $\Psi = 0$ and $\eta = 1.00001$.

The first and simplest approach to evaluate the increase in particle temperature during condensation is to assume that the vapor concentration at the surface of the particle is un influenced by the change in the particle temperature. Results obtained through this assumption are the upper limit of the real situation. Then, if the increase in temperature is minimum $\delta T \ll 1$, the model would prove that the assumption of constant temperature is a good assumption. If that is not the case, the temperature dependence of vapor phase concentration at the surface of the particle needs to be included.

Equations (3) and (5) were solved numerically for different values of the parameter $\xi_{CR,}$ assuming that the rate of condensation is uninfluenced by the increase in particle temperature. The actual increase in particle temperature is determined by the parameter ξ_{CR} and ζ. $1/\zeta$ is the fraction of the energy released that is used to increase the particle temperature, while ξ_{CR} is the ratio of the energy dissipated by conduction and the energy required to increase particle temperature. Higher values of ξ_{CR} means that more energy can be dissipated per degree of particle temperature increased, and therefore lower δTs for the same rate of energy release.

For NaCl at 1100°C, ζ=7650.1. Table 2 shows typical values for $\xi_{CR.}$ For these values, Figure 1 shows the increase in particle temperature during NaCl condensation in the CR. Figure 1 shows that particle heating is a function of particle size. These can be explained as follows: At any given time, a gradient of temperature $\delta T = T_p - T_\infty$ is established such that the rate of energy dissipation by convection, which is proportional to δT, balances the rate of heat release. The rate of heat release is proportional to the rate of condensation. In the CR, the rate of condensation is a function of particle size. Consequently, temperature increase in the CR is a function of particle size.

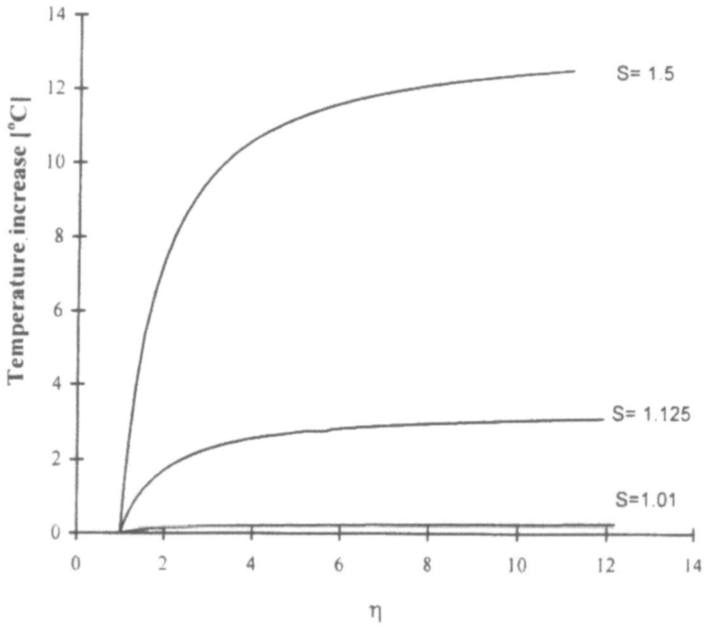

Figure 1. Increase in particle temperature during NaCl condensation in the CR for different values of S assuming that the rate of condensation is uninfluenced by the increase in particle temperature.

Table 2 shows the increase in temperature when the particle has grown 10 times its initial size by condensation. δT is small for S<1.5 and therefore it can be concluded that the assumption of constant temperature during condensation of NaCl in the CR is acceptable for low rates of condensation.

http://dx.doi.org/10.5772/62017

S	ξ_{CR}	Ψ_{10}	δT
1.010	2.82×10^4	3.18×10^{-5}	0.24
1.125	2.14×10^3	3.99×10^{-4}	3.05
1.500	4.65×10^2	1.62×10^{-3}	12.4

Table 2. Temperature increase during condensation in the CR. For NaCl particles starting with size r* and ending with 10 times their initial size, assuming that the rate of condensation is unaffected by the increase in particle temperature.

Heat Transfer in the FMR

Particle heating during condensation in the FMR is enhanced because thermal conduction in the FMR is not as good as in the CR. Conduction of heat in the FMR follows very different laws from those obeyed under ordinary circumstances. References 84, 85, 86, and 87 are frequently used references in this respect.

Expressions for thermal conduction from a single sphere toward its environment in stagnant conditions are obtained from the kinetic theory of gases. On it, the area surrounding the particle is divided in two zones. The inner zone is of the width of one mean free path, and transport occurs at collisionless rates. This is known as the Langmuir zone. At larger distances, transport processes involve many collisions and follow the CR description. The heat flux due to conduction across the Langmuir layer is given by [84]:

$$\frac{q}{A\delta T} = \frac{1}{2}(\gamma+1)\frac{C_v P}{\sqrt{\frac{2\pi RT}{M}}} = \frac{K_k}{r} \tag{6}$$

where A is surface area, q is heat flux, $\gamma = C_p/C_v$ is the ratio of specific heat capacities, and K_k is an equivalent thermal conductivity as given by the kinetic theory. Equation (6) states that in the FMR, conduction is proportional to the pressure of the gas, and dependent only upon shape but not size of the bounding surfaces.

Replacing the conduction term of Equation (1) by the expression for conduction in the FMR (Equation (6)), the energy balance for condensation in the FMR is:

$$\frac{d\Psi}{d\tau} = \frac{1}{\eta}\frac{d\eta}{d\tau} - \xi\frac{\Psi}{\eta} \tag{7}$$

$$\xi = \frac{3MK_k\tau_{cond}}{\rho C_p r^*} \tag{8}$$

and the condensation rate in the FMR is:

$$\frac{d\eta}{d\tau} = \frac{1}{Ln(S)}\left(1 - S^{\frac{1}{\eta}-1}\right) \tag{9}$$

where the same type of nondimensionalization has been used as for the CR case. Figure 2 shows the numerical solution of Equations (7) and (9) subject to the initial conditions $\Psi = O$ and $\eta = 1.00001$. Again it has been assumed that particle heating does not affect the rate of condensation.

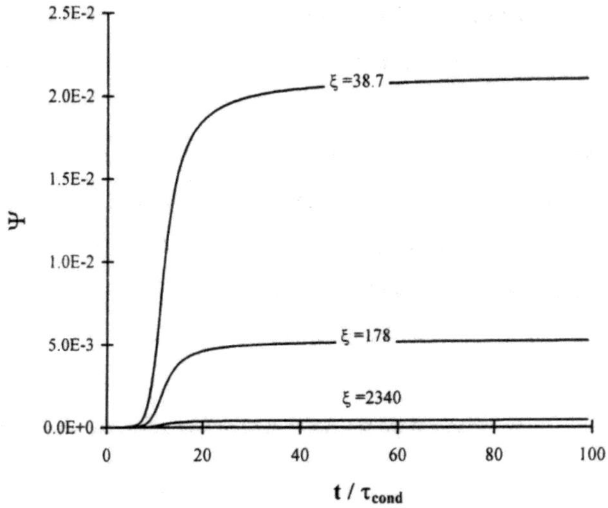

Figure 2. Increase in particle temperature during condensation in the FMR for different values of ξ assuming that the rate of condensation is uninfluenced by the increase in particle temperature.

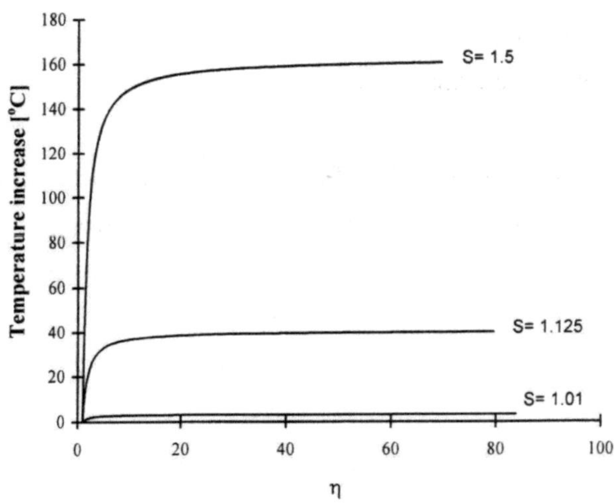

Figure 3. Actual particle temperature increase during condensation of NaCl at 1100°C in the FMR. For different saturation ratios, assuming that the rate is uninfluenced by the increase in particle temperature.

http://dx.doi.org/10.5772/62017

Figure 2 shows that the nondimensional temperature reaches a steady-state value Ψ_∞. This steady-state condition is reached when the Kelvin effect ceases and the rate of condensation becomes constant. This behavior can be explained in the following way.

At any time during condensation, a gradient of temperature $\delta T = T_p - T_\infty$ is established such that the rate of energy dissipation, which is proportional to δT, balances the rate of heat release, which is proportional to the rate of condensation. During condensation controlled by the Kelvin effect, the rate of condensation is a function of particle size and then the temperature of the particle is also a function of particle size. However, when the particles grow, the Kelvin effect becomes negligible and the rate of condensation independent of particle size. Consequently, despite further condensation, the particles reach and maintain a constant temperature.

Equation (3) shows the actual increase in particle temperature for several conditions of super saturation of NaCl at 1100°C. It shows that even for low values of S, the increase of particle temperature is substantial. Therefore, a heat transfer analysis that includes the effect of particle heating on the rate of condensation is required.

Saturation pressure can be expressed as $P_s = a^*T^n$, where a and n are constants. Then the saturation ratio can be expressed as $S=S_\infty(T/T_\infty)^n$,where the subscript ∞ refers to the properties of the aerosol far away from the particle. Properties at ∞ are assumed to be constant.

$(T/T_\infty)^n$ can be expressed in terms of $\delta T/T_\infty=(T_p-T_\infty)/T_\infty$ by expanding it in Taylor series and neglecting higher-order terms. The resulting expression is $S=S\infty*Exp(-n\,\delta T/T\infty)$. In terms of the nondimensional variable Ψ and ζ:

$$S = S_\infty * Exp(-n\zeta\Psi) \tag{10}$$

Incorporating this expression into the energy and condensation equation, nondimensionalizing in the same fashion as before but with respect to the properties at ∞, the energy and condensation equations become:

$$\frac{d\Psi}{d\tau} = \frac{1}{\eta}\frac{d\eta}{d\tau} - \xi\frac{\Psi}{\eta} \tag{11}$$

$$\frac{d\eta}{d\tau} = \frac{1}{Ln(S_\infty)} Exp\left(-\frac{\gamma\Psi}{2T_\infty}\right)\left[1-\left(S_\infty * Exp\left(\frac{-n\gamma\Psi}{T_\infty}\right)\right)^{\frac{1}{\eta}-1}\right] \tag{12}$$

Now the condensation equation is coupled to the energy equation and vice versa. Figure 4 shows the results after integrating simultaneously the two equations subject to the initial conditions $\Psi = O$ and $\eta = 1.00001$, for $\zeta/T_\infty = 5.57$ and the values of ξ corresponding to S = 1.01, 1.125, and 1.5.

The behavior of the particle temperature is similar to that already described, except that the steady-state temperature is ~4 times less. Table 3 compares the values obtained with and

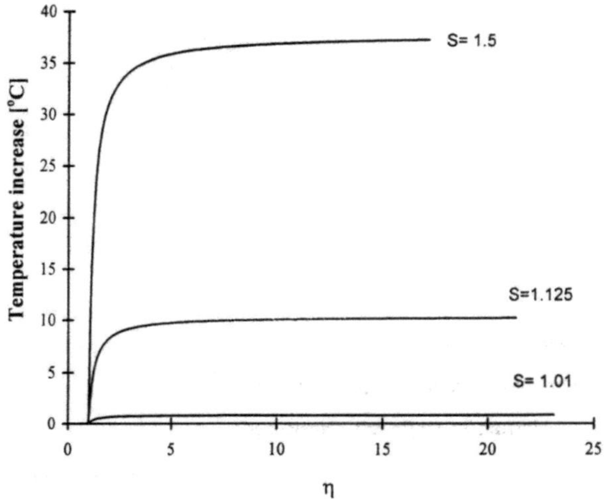

Figure 4. NaCl condensation in the FMR for different values of S including the effect of particle heating in the rate of condensation.

without correction for temperature. It shows that particle heating due to condensation is substantial for higher values of S_∞.

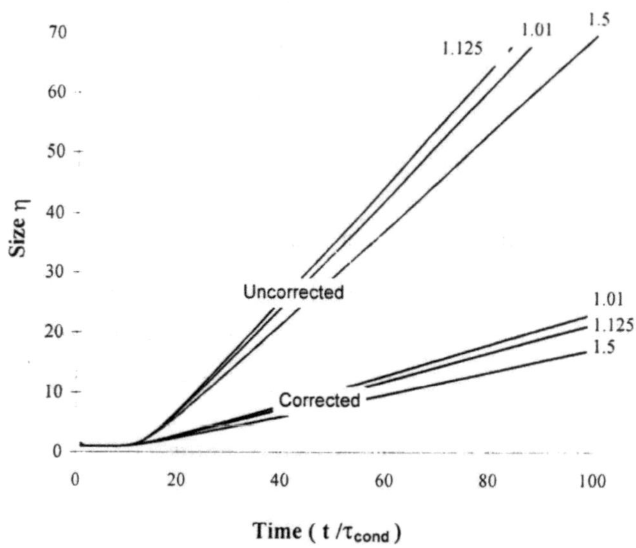

Figure 5. Effect of particle heating on particle growth.

Figure 5 shows the effect of particle heating on particle growth. It shows that particle growth has the same profile with and without correction for temperature; however, particle heating decreases the rate of growth by a factor of ~4. Then, clearly the effect of particle heating on the rate of condensation in the FMR is important.

http://dx.doi.org/10.5772/62017

S_∞	ξ	τ_{cond}	m	δT	$m_{w/o}/m$	$\delta T_{w/o}/\delta T$
1.01	2340	2.71×10^{-3}	0.25	0.81	3.92	3.8
1.125	178	1.74×10^{-5}	0.23	9.86	4.03	3.9
1.5	38.7	1.10×10^{-6}	0.18	37.5	4.49	4.3

m = rate of condensation in the FMR when the Kelvin effect becomes ineffective

w/o = without correction for particle heating

Table 3. Values for condensation in the FMR with correction for particle heating.

Figure 5 can be used to evaluate particle growth in the FMR for any starting size and a given δt by using:

$$\delta\eta = \int_{t_o}^{t_o+\delta t} \frac{d\eta}{dt} dt = \int_{0}^{t_o+\delta t} \frac{d\eta}{dt} dt - \int_{0}^{t_o} \frac{d\eta}{dt} dt \tag{13}$$

$$\delta\eta = \eta_{0-\tau_o+\delta t} - \eta_{0-\tau_o} \tag{14}$$

where $\eta_{o\text{-}\tau}$ is the tabulated universal value for growth due to condensation during τ nondimensional times. Equation (13) is in general not valid because condensation is coupled to the energy equation. Particle growth depends on the particle temperature and in general particles of the same size could have different temperatures.

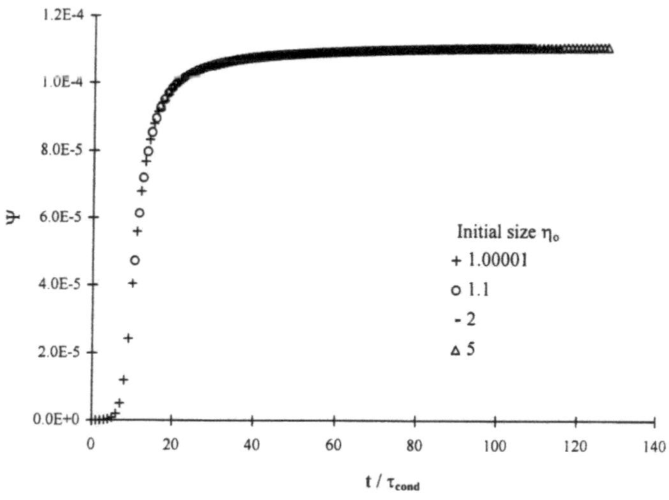

Figure 6. Particle temperature and size for the same conditions but different initial size. Particles of the same size have the same temperature.

However, for situations where $\zeta \ll 1$ and $Bi \ll 1$, as in the case of NaCl condensation over nanosize particles, Equation 13 is still valid because a) the amount of energy required to heat up the particle is negligible compared to the energy available ($\zeta \ll 1$) and b) the rate of particle heating is instantaneous ($Bi \ll 1$). Therefore, particles of the same size have the same temperature regardless of how much condensation was received, as long as there has been some condensation. Figure 6 shows this behavior. For the same conditions but different initial size, particle temperature is only a function of particle size.

2. Appendix B

2.1. Sintering

The theory of sintering of solid particles or highly viscous fluids is based in the interaction of two equal-sized spheres. At the contact point of the two spheres, a neck is formed whose size grows with time. For the initial stage, the rate of growth is driven by the curvature gradients in the neck region. At intermediate sintering rates, the curvature gradient diminishes and the surface free energy becomes the driving force for continued sintering. At this stage, the motion is induced by the tendency of the interface to reduce its area in order to minimize the interfacial energy. [88]

For the initial stage of the sintering process, the kinetic model formulated by Frenkel 89 and generalized by German and Muir [88] has shown good agreement with experimental values obtained during sintering studies of various materials. On it, the rate of surface area reduction is given by:

$$\frac{da}{dt} \sim -\frac{1}{\tau_f}(a - a_f)^{\gamma - 1} \tag{15}$$

where a is the surface area of the aggregate, a_f the surface area of the completely fused single sphere of the same volume, γ is a constant, and τ_f is the characteristic fusion time. The values of γ and τ_f depend on the underlying sintering mechanism. Table 1 shows some of the possible sintering mechanism and values of γ for each of them.

Hiram and Nir [90] developed a numerical solution for the equations of motion describing the coalescence of two particles by the viscous flow mechanism. The results show similar behavior for all particle size to fluid viscosity ratios. The sintering behavior displays three regions of evolution: an initial transitory stage followed by an intermediate pseudo-Frenkel stage. Beyond these two short states, particles assume their spherical shape following a first-order exponential decay.

http://dx.doi.org/10.5772/62017

$$\frac{da}{dt} \sim -\frac{1}{\tau_f}(a - a_f) \quad (16)$$

In this case, the characteristic time for coalescence τ_f is the time required to reduce 63% the excess agglomerate surface area over that of a spherical particle with the same mass.

Koch and Friedlander [91] assumed that the linear growth rate, Equation (1), holds for the solid-state diffusion mechanism, and obtained an expression for τ_f. Table 1 shows the type of expressions obtained and some of the expressions used by several authors in the study of gas phase particle synthesis when coalescence is the rate-controlling process. On this type of work, the authors assume that the very small particles grow by single particle collision and almost instantaneously coalesce until they become large enough to exhibit macroscopic viscosity and surface tension.

For the rate of sintering of Ti at $T<T_m$, it is assumed that the rate of sintering is due to solid-state diffusion. Since information about self-diffusion as a function of temperature is not available for Ti, the respective information for C in HCP Ti has been used [92] as a first approximation. The values obtained are reported in Table 2. The results show that the rate of sintering of Ti is high up to particles of size r~10 nm, but it is a strong function of temperature. The rate of sintering by viscous flow is reported in Table 2 for NaCl. It shows that liquid NaCl particles sinter extremely fast.

Mechanism	Equation (1)		Equation (2)		
	γ	$\delta\gamma$	τ_f	Material	Expression Used
Viscous	1.1	± 0.1	$\frac{2\mu r_f}{\sigma}$ [89]	SiO_2 [93]	$6.5x10^{15}$ d Exp($8.3x10^4$/T)
Evaporation/Condensation	1.6	± 0.1	$\frac{3KTv}{64\pi D\sigma v_m}$ [94]		
Solid-state diffusion					
Volume diffusion	2.7	± 0.1		B_4C [95]	39 T d^3 Exp(53 648/T)
Grain boundary diffusion	3.3	± 0.1		TiO_2 [93]	$7.4x10^8$ T d^4 Exp($3.1x10^4$/T)
Surface diffusion	3.6	± 0.1			

T absolute temperature

v particle volume

D solid-state diffusion coefficient

d particle diameter of the sintered particle

σ surface tension

v_m molecular volume

Table 4. Sintering mechanisms and different expressions for the characteristic time.

Size r [nm]	τ_{sint} [μs]			
	1100°C		800 °C	
	Ti (c)	NaCl (l)	Ti (c)	NaCl (l)
3.8	1.21×10^{-2}	3.73×10^{-4}	4.14×10^{-1}	3.18×10^{-3}
5.9	4.48×10^{-2}	5.78×10^{-3}	1.55×10^{0}	4.94×10^{-3}
15.0	7.11×10^{-1}	1.45×10^{-2}	2.55×10^{1}	1.26×10^{-2}
50.0	2.70×10^{1}	4.88×10^{-2}	9.44×10^{2}	4.19×10^{-2}
100.0	2.16×10^{2}	9.77×10^{-2}	7.55×10^{3}	8.37×10^{-2}

Table 5. Characteristic time for sintering of Ti particles in crystal phase and NaCl in liquid phase at 1100°C.

3. Appendix C

3.1. Particle Dynamics in a Colloidal System

A colloid is an entity dispersed in a medium, having at least one dimension between 1 nm and 1 μm. The entity may be solid or liquid or, in some cases, even gaseous. A solid colloid dispersed in a liquid medium is known as sol or dispersion. However, the term "colloid" is generally used for the system as a whole.[96, 97]

Particles in a liquid medium possess Brownian motion and therefore eventually collide. The theory of coagulation due to Brownian motion may be applied to the colloidal system to determine how fast the particles collide. The resistance of the liquid phase to the motion of a spherical particle is proportional to the size of the particle and the hydrodynamic nature of the liquid phase. That relation is well known as the Stokes formula:

$$F_{M=-6\pi\mu rV} \tag{17}$$

where μ is the viscosity of the fluid, r is the particle size, and V is the particle velocity. The ratio of the velocity of the particle V to the force causing its motion F_M is called mobility (B) of the particle. B is the drift velocity that is attained under unit external force. In some other areas the quantity $f=1/B=6\pi\mu r$. It is more popular and it is known as the Stokes friction coefficient. On the other hand, the diffusivity (D) of a particle of size r_i in the liquid medium is given by:

$$D_i = \frac{KT}{f_i} \tag{18}$$

and the collision frequency function β is given by:

http://dx.doi.org/10.5772/62017

$$\beta = 4\pi(D_i + D_j)(r_i + r_j) \tag{19}$$

Finally, the collision frequency of the solid particles in the colloidal system is given by:

$$Z_{ij} = \beta_{ij} n_i n_j \tag{20}$$

where N◎ is the concentration of particles of size r◎. Replacing Equations 1, 2, and 3 in Equation 4, an explicit expression for the frequency of collision can be obtained. Considering a colloidal system, made of two equal-sized particles (r) embedded in a liquid droplet of size R, the characteristic collision time τB =N/Z reduces to:

$$\tau_B = \frac{\mu \pi R^3}{8KT} \tag{21}$$

The characteristic collision time τ_B for the colloidal system estimates the average time required for two particles to collide. This definition neglects the enhancing effect in the collision frequency of having the two particles housed within the boundaries of the liquid material. However, it gives a good first estimate. τ_B is independent of particle size, and is linearly proportional to the volume available for particle motion. For NaCl at 800°C and 1100°C, Table 1 shows typical values for τ_B.

NaCl droplet Size R [nm]	τ_B [μs]	
	1100°C	800°C
10	9.38×10^{-1}	1.27×10^{0}
25	1.47×10^{1}	1.98×10^{1}
50	1.17×10^{2}	1.58×10^{2}
100	9.38×10^{2}	1.27×10^{3}

Table 6. Characteristic time for collision of 2 Ti cores embedded within a NaCl liquid droplet of size R.

Author details

Jose Ignacio Huertas

Address all correspondence to: jhuertas@itesm.mx

Tecnológico de Monterrey, Mexico

References

[1] Suryanarayana, C., and Froes, F.H. *Metallu Trans A.* 23A:1071-1081. (1992).

[2] Birringuer, R. Nanocrystalline Materials. *Mater Sci Engin A.* 117:33-43. (1989).

[3] Gleiter, H. Materials with Ultrafine Microstructures: Retrospectives and Perspectives. *Nano Struct Mater.* 1:1-19. (1992).

[4] Cohen, M. Progress and Prospects in Metallurgical Research. *Advancing Material Research.* Washington D.C. Pp. 51-110. (1987).

[5] Gleiter, H. *Progr Mater Sci.* 33:223-315. (1989).

[6] Nieman, G.W., Weertman, J.R., and Siegel, R.W. *Scri. Metal.* 24:145. (1990).

[7] Suryanarayana, C., and Froes, F.H. Nanocrystalline Metals: A Review. *Physical Chemistry of Powder Metals. Production and Processing.* Pp. 279-296. (1989).

[8] Courtney, T.H. *Mechanical Behavior of Materials.* McGraw-Hill. New York. (1990).

[9] Birringer, R., Bohn, R.W., and Weertman, J.R., *Mater Sci Engin A.* 153:679. (1993).

[10] Nieman, G.W., Siegel, R.W., and Weertman, J.R. *J Mater Res.* 6:1012. (1991).

[11] Siegel, R.W., and Hahn, H. Current Trends in Physic of Materials. In *World Scientific.* Singapore. Pp. 403. (1987).

[12] Ashley, S. Small-Scale Structure Yields Big Property Payoffs. *Mechanical Engineering.* February. Pp. 52-57. (1994).

[13] Stiglich, J.J., Sudarshan, T.S., and Dowding, R.J. *Synthesis and Consolidation of Nanoparticles.* U.S. Army Research Laboratory. AD-A238 314. (1994).

[14] Simon, C. Stabilization of Aqueous Powder Suspensions in the Processing of Ceramic Materials and Advanced Materials, in *Coagulation and Flocculation, Theory and Applications.* Ed. Dobias, B., Marcel. D. Inc. New York. Pp. 487. (1993).

[15] Niihara, K. *Cera Soc Jpn.* 99:974. (1991).

[16] Zachariah, M.R. Principles of Gas Phase Processing of Ceramics During Combustion. Pp. 71-76. (1994).

[17] Kingery, W.D., Bowen, H.K., and Uhlmann, D.R. *Introduction to Ceramics.* Wiley. New York. (1976).

[18] Matteazzi, P. Basset, D., Miani, F., and Le-Caer, G. Mechanosynthesis of Nanophase Materials. *Nanostr Mater.* 2:217-229. (1993).

[19] Gurav, A., Kodas, T., Pluym, T., and Xiong Y. Aerosol Processing of Materials. *Aerosol Sci Technol.* 19:411-452. (1993).

http://dx.doi.org/10.5772/62017

[20] Uyeda, R. Studies of Ultrafine Particles in Japan: Crystallography, Methods of Preparation and Technological Applications. *Progr Mater Sci.* 35:1-96. (1991).

[21] Chorley, R.W., and Lednor, P.W. Synthetic Routes to High Surface Area Non-Oxide Materials. *Adv Mater.* 3:10:474-485. (1991).

[22] Lamprey, H., and Ripley, R.L., *J Electrochem Soc.* 109:8:713-715. (1962).

[23] Pratsinis, S.E., and Kodas, T.T., Manufacturing of Materials by Aerosol Processes. In *Aerosol Measurement: Principles, Techniques, and Applications.* Pp. 721-746. (1993).

[24] Flagan, R.C., and Wu, J.J. Aerosol Reactor Production of Uniform Submicron Powders. *Patent No. 248486.* (1991).

[25] Zachariah, M.R., and Dimitriou, P. *Aerosol Sc Technol.* 13:413-425. (1990).

[26] Axelbaum, R.L., DuFaux, O.P., and Rosen, L.J. *Patent No. 5498446.* (1995).

[27] Magness, L.S., and Farrand T.G. *Army Science Conference.* (1990).

[28] Ryan, K.F., and Dowding, R.J. *Army Research Laboratories.*ARL-TR-143. (1993).

[29] Schubert, W.D. *Refractory Metals and Hard Materials.* 11:151-157. (1992).

[30] Williams, B.E., Stiglich, J.J., and Kaplan R.B. Coated Tungsten Powders For Advance Ordinance Applications. *US Army Materials Technology Laboratory.* MTL TR. Pp. 92. (1992).

[31] German, R.M., Tungsten and Tungsten Alloys. *Proceedings of the First International Conference on Tungsten and Tungsten Alloys.* Metal Powder Industry Federation. New Jersey. Pp. 3. (1993).

[32] Raghunathan, S., Bourell, D.L., and Persad, C. Microcomposites and Nanophase Materials. *The Minerals, Metals & Materials Society.* Pp. 81. (1991).

[33] Kecskes, L.J., and Hall, I.W. *Proceedings of the First International Conference on Tungsten and Tungsten Alloys.* Metal Powder Industry Federation. New Jersey. Pp. 155. (1993).

[34] Hessel, S., Shpigler, B., and Botstein, O. *Rev Chem Engin.* 9:3-4:345-364. (1993).

[35] Kear, B.H., and McCandlish, L.E. *J Adv Mater.* October. Pp.11-19. (1993).

[36] Currie, A.L., and Howard, K.E. *J Mater Sci.* 27:2739-2742. (1992).

[37] Belkacem, A., Arnal, Y., and Pelletier, J. *Thin Solid Films.* 241:301-304. (1994).

[38] Evans, R. D., and Leet, D.M. *J Electrochem Soc.* 141: 7:1867-1871. (1994).

[39] Hojo, J., Oku, T., and Kato, A. *J Less Common Metals.* 59:85-95 (1978).

[40] Smiley, S.H., Brater, D.C., and Kaufman, H.L. *J Metals.* June. Pp. 605. (1965).

[41] Revankar, V., Zhao, G.Y., and Hlavacek, V. *Ind Eng. Chem. Res.* 30:2344. (1991).

[42] DuFaux, O.P., and Axelbaum, R.L. *Combust Flame.* 100:350-358. (1995).

[43] Axelbaun, R.L., Lottes, C.R., Huertas, J.I., and Rosen L. To be published in *Twenty-Fifth Symposium International on Combustion.* (1996).

[44] Gould, R.K., and Dickson, C.R. *Patent No. 5021221.* (1991).

[45] Calcote, H.F., and Felder, W. *Twenty-Fourth Symposium International on Combustion.* Pp.1869-1876 (1994).

[46] Glassman, I, Davis, K.A., and Brezinsky, K. *Twenty-Fourth International Symposium on Combustion.* Pp. 1-14. (1994).

[47] Steffens, K.L., Zacbariah, M.R., DuFaux, D.P., and Axelbawn, R.L. To be published. (1996).

[48] Massalski, T.B. *Binary Alloys Phase Diagrams.*2nd Ed. New York. (1990).

[49] Cullity, B.O. *Elements of X-ray diffraction.* 2nd Ed. MA. (1977).

[50] Friedlander, S.K. *Smoke, Dust and Haze.* John Wiley & Sons. New York. (1977).

[51] Suck, S.H, and Brock, J.R. *J Aerosol Sci.* 10:581-590. (1979).

[52] Friedlander, S.K., and Wang, C.S. The Self-Preserving Particle Size Distribution for Coagulation by Brownian Motion. *J Colloid Interf Sci.* 22:126-132. (1966).

[53] Lee, K.W., Chen, H., and Gieseke, J.A. *Aerosol Sci Technol.* 3:53 (1984).

[54] Gelbard, F., Tambour, Y., and Seinfeld, J.H. Sectional Representations for Simulating Aerosol Dynamics. *J Colloid Interf Sci.* 76:2:541-556. (1979).

[55] Husar, R.B. *Coagulation of Knudsen Aerosols.* Ph.D. dissertation. University of Minnesota. (1971).

[56] Kaplan, C.R., and Gentry, J.W. Agglomeration of Chain-Like Combustion Aerosols Due to Brownian Motion. *Aerosol Sci Technol.* 8:11-28. (1988).

[57] Gelbard, F., and Seinfeld, J.H. *J Colloid Interf Sci.* 68:363. (1979).

[58] Gelbard, F., and Seinfeld, J.H. Simulation of Multicomponent Aerosol Dynamics. *J Colloid Interf Sci.* 78:2:485-501. (1980).

[59] Tsang, T.H. and Rao, A. Comparison of Different Numerical Schemes for Condensational Growth of Aerosols. *Aerosol Sci Technol.* 9:271-277. (1988).

[60] Warren, D.R. and Seinfeld, J.H. Simulation of Aerosol Size Distribution Evolution in Systems with Simultaneous Nucleation, Condensation, and Coagulation. *Aerosol Sci Technol.* 4:31-43. (1985).

[61] Gelbard, F. Modeling Multicomponent Aerosol Particle Growth by Vapor Condensation. *Aerosol Sci Technol.* 12:399-412. (1990).

http://dx.doi.org/10.5772/62017

[62] Jacobson, M.Z., and Turco, R.P. Simulating Condensational Growth, Evaporation.and Coagulation of Aerosols Using a Combined Moving and Stationary Size Grid. *Aerosol Sci Technol.* 22:73-92. (1995).

[63] Gelbard, F., and Seinfeld, J. Exact Solution of the General Dynamic Equation for Aerosol Growth by Condensation. *J Colloid Interf Sci.* 28:1:173-183. (1978).

[64] Seinfeld, J.H. *Atmospheric Chemistry and Physics of Air Pollution.* John Wiley & Sons. New York. (1986).

[65] Siegel, R., and Howell, J.R. *Thermal Radiation Heat Transfer.* 2nd Ed. Washington. (1981).

[66] Shreider, Y.A. *The Monte Carlo Method* Pergamon Press. New York. (1966).

[67] Schaad, L.J. The Monte Carlo Integration of Rate Equations. *J Am Cera Soc.* 85:3588-3592. (1963).

[68] Kaplan, C.R., and Gentry, J.W. Agglomeration of Chain-Like Combustion Aerosols due to Brownian Motion. *Aerosol Sci Technol.* 8:11-28. (1988).

[69] Akhtar, M.K, Lippscomb, G.G., and Pratsinis, S.E. Monte Carlo Simulation of Particle Coagulation and Sintering. *Aerosol Sci Technol.* 21:83-93 (1994).

[70] Sutherland, D.N. A Theoretical Model of Floc Structures. *J Colloid Interf Sci.* 25; 373-380. (1967).

[71] Kemeny, J.G, and Snell, J.L *Finite Markov Chains.* New York. (1960).

[72] Levine, J., Levine, M., Negus, C., and Schumer, L. *The UNIX Dictionary of Commands, Terms and Acronyms.* McGraw-Hill. NewYork. (1996).

[73] Hidy, G. M. On the Theory of the Coagulation of Noninteracting Particles in Brownian Motion. *J Colloid Sci.* 20:123-144. (1964).

[74] Lee, K.W., Curtís, L.A. and Chen, H. An Analytic Solution to the Free Molecule Aerosol Coagulation. *Aerosol Sci Technol.* 12:457-462. (1990).

[75] Matsoukas, T. and Friedlander, S.K. Dynamics of Aerosol Agglomerate Formation. *J Colloid Interf Sci.* 146:2. (1991).

[76] Megaridis, C. Morphological Description of Flame generated Materials. *Combust Sci Technol.*71:95-109. (1990).

[77] Akhtar, M.K., Xiong, Y., and Pratsinis, S.E. Vapor Synthesis of Titania Powder by Titanium Tretachloride Oxidation. *AlChE J.* 37:10:1561-1570. (1991).

[78] Law, A.M., and Kelton, W.D. *Simulation Modeling and Analysis.* 2nd Ed. McGraw-Hill. New York. (1991).

[79] Abraham, F.F. *Homogeneous Nucleation Theory.* Academic Press. New York. (1974).

[80] MacDonald. *Am J Phys.* 30:12:870-877. (1962).

[81] MacDonald. *Am J Phys.* 31:1:31-41. (1963).

[82] German, R.M. and Munir, Z.A. Surface Area Reduction During Isothermal Sintering, *JAm Cera Soc.* 59:9-10. (1976).

[83] Dukhin, S.S., Kretzschmar, G., and Mil1er, R. *Dynamics of Adsorption at Liquid Interfaces.* Elsevier. The Netherlands. (1995).

[84] Kennard, E.H. *Kinetic Theory of Gases.* McGraw-Hill. New York. (1938).

[85] Chapman, S and Cowling, T.G. *The Mathematical Theory of Non-Uniform Gases.* Cambridge University Press. London (1970).

[86] Eckbreth, A.C. Effect of Laser-Modulated Particle Incandescence on Raman Scattering Diagnostics. *J Appl Phys.* 48:11:4473-4479. (1977).

[87] McCoy, B.J. and Cha, C.Y. Transport Phenomena in the Rarefied Gas Transition Regime. *Chem Engin Sci.*29:381-388. (1974).

[88] German, R.M. and MWlir, Z.A. Surface Area Reduction During Isothermal Sintering, *J Am Cera Soc.*59:9-10. (1976).

[89] Frenkel, J. *J Phys.* 9:385. (1945).

[90] Hiram, Y and Nir, A. A Simulation of Surface Tension Driven Coalescence. *J Colloid Interf Sci.* 95:2:462-470. (1983).

[91] Koch, W and Friedlander, S.K. The Effect of Particle Coalescence on the Surface Area of a Coagulating Aerosol, *J Colloid Interf Sci.* 140:2:419-427. (1990).

[92] Van Vlack, L.H. *Elements of Material Science and Engineering.* 5th Ed. Adison-Wesley. New York. (1985).

[93] Xiong, Y., Akhtar K., and Pratsinis, S.E. Formation of Agglomerate Particles by Coagulation and Sintering- Part 11. The Evolution of the Morphology of Aerosol-Made Titania, Silica, and Silica Doped Titania Powders. *J Aerosol Sci.*24:3:310-313. (1993).

[94] Friedlander, S.K., and Wu, M.K. Linear Rate Law for the Decay of the Excess Surface Area of a Coalescing Solid Particle. *Phys Rev B.* 49:3622-3624. (1994).

[95] Xiong, Y., Pratsinis, S.E., and Weimer, A.W. Modeling the Formation of Boron Carbide Particles in an Aerosol Flow Reactor. *AIChE J.* 38:11:1685-1692. (1992)

[96] Lyklema, J. *Fundamentals of Interface and Colloid Science.* Vol. l. Academic Press. New York. (1991).

[97] Hunter, R.J. *Foundations of Colloid Science.* Vol. 1. Clarendon Press. New York. (1987).

[98] Hinds, W.C. Physical and Chemical Changes in Particulate Phase. In *Aerosol Measurements, Principles, Techniques and Applications.* Ed. Willeke, K., and Baron, P.A. John Wiley and Sons. New York (1994).